Linda Whitney Peterson, Ph.D., has been a tenured associate professor of pediatrics and psychiatry at the University of Nevada School of Medicine since 1978. In her private practice, Dr. Peterson works with children suffering from acute and chronic illness, PTSD and bereavement issues. As a custody evaluator/arbitrator, she specializes in forensic medicine with court consultation regarding custody and sexual and physical abuse cases.

Milton Edward Hardin, M.A., is a child advocacy counselor at the Family Center of the Conciliation Court of Pima county, Tucson, Arizona. With twenty years of experience, he is considered an expert in custody evaluations and court testimony as well as consultations to parents regarding children of divorce. His research and areas of interest are child sexual abuse and cultural diversity.

CHILDREN IN DISTRESS

A Guide for Screening Children's Art

A NORTON PROFESSIONAL BOOK

CHILDREN IN DISTRESS

A Guide for Screening
Children's Art

LINDA WHITNEY PETERSON
MILTON EDWARD HARDIN

W. W. NORTON & COMPANY
New York • London

Printed in the United States of America
First Edition

For information about permission to reproduce selections from this book write to
Permissions, W.W. Norton & Company, Inc.
500 Fifth Avenue, New York, NY 10110

Library of Congress Cataloging-in-Publication Data

Peterson, Linda Whitney.
  Children in distress : a guide for screening children's art / Linda Whitney
Peterson, Milton Edward Hardin.
     p.   cm.
  "Norton Professional book."
  Includes bibliographical references.
  ISBN 0-393-70248-0 (spiral bound)
  1. Children's drawings — Psychological aspects. 2. Projective techniques for
children. I. Hardin, Milton Edward. II. Title.
RJ503.7.P76P48   1997
618.92'89075—dc21   97-3930
                                                  CIP

W.W. Norton & Company, Inc., 500 Fifth Avenue, New York, NY 10110
http://www.wwnorton.com
W.W. Norton & Company Ltd., 10 Coptic Street, London WC1A 1PU

1 2 3 4 5 6 7 8 9 0

Acknowledgments

This book is dedicated to the children who have shared their art work with me over 25 years in clinics, schools, hospitals, homes and courts. I regret there were some pictures I could not decipher. I thank Dr. Jack Lazerson, of the Department of Pediatrics at the University of Nevada Medical School, who said: "Follow your heart" and "Focus on this work." I applaud Milton Hardin who in spite of a debilitating disease assisted me to develop the scoring forms in this manuscript for both the human figure and kinetic family drawings. His research with 842 children substantiates art markers so clinicians will not miss what a child is communicating through drawing. "Teddy" Swecker redrew all my collected child pictures so readers could learn without the distraction of different child formats. It was she who said: "I have the feeling these children are trying so hard to be happy." Dr. Monica Nitsch wisely assisted me with her technical skills so "physicians will remember art in the practice of medicine." Dr. Richard Rahe, my friend and mentor, added his editorial expertise. Finally I acknowledge you, the reader, for the emotional energy it takes to view what these children are exposing in their art work. Only as we appreciate these expressions, and say "thank you," rather than denying or feeling sorry, can we heal the children and ourselves.

— *Linda Whitney Peterson*

There are many people who have selflessly aided me in the project that culminated in this book, but there are seven people who deserve special acknowledgment. First, I would like to acknowledge Kathy Milbeck, M.A., who was there from the beginning and whose work with molested children was the inspiration for my research. Next, I would like to acknowledge Ruth Ann Kishi and Elizabeth Wong Hardin. Without their hard work and companionship, the original research study would not have been completed. I would like to acknowledge Duane Varble, Ph.D., whose direction and assistance allowed me to develop a study worthy of his high professional standards. I would also like to acknowledge Linda Q. Kerr, M.S., and David Gooden, A.C.S.W., whose continued friendship and encouragement helped me to see that I still could be productive. And last, but most importantly, I acknowledge Linda Peterson, Ph.D., whose patience and perseverance were the real driving forces behind this book. She is a very special woman and I am blessed for having the opportunity to work with her.

—*Milton Edward Hardin*

I dedicate this book to the already perfect light in every child.
Shine brightly.

—*Theodocia Swecker*

Contents

Figures and Tables

Introduction

Dr. S. swiveled uncomfortably on a chair in his office at the Special Children's Clinic. He noticed a perceptible pain in his gut. He was holding a picture handed to him by the clinic psychologist, which had been spontaneously scribbled by the child he had just examined. Susan was a $3\frac{1}{2}$-year-old child, brought by her grandmother who reported a sudden change in the personality of the child including clingy behavior and tantrums as well as nightmares and persistent talk about a "puppet man" entering her bedroom at night. The grandmother expressed concern about the lifestyle of the mother and was suspicious of the new stepfather.

This pediatrician had examined children for 25 years. He was the leading regional expert in the evaluation of physical and sexual abuse, as well the best teacher and administrator in the department of pediatrics of a medical school. He was respected by the professional community and loved by children and parents alike. But try as he might, he could not get Susan to do any more than make vague references to a puppet man in her bedroom. The child's physical, including colposcopic exam was normal, but her demeanor and her drawing worried him. He consulted with his peers to see if they could identify anything he might have missed. Not a lot had been written regarding the evaluation of potential victims of sexual molestation at the time. In fact, his use of the colposcope was the state of the art assessment at the time. Hibbard and associates had not yet reported their research in the *Journal of Pediatrics* on the significance of child drawings of explicit genitalia. Clearly the picture the doctor held in his hand was the rendering of a large male phallus, scratched over with purple and black crayon. It was the sole communication that had transpired between the physician and the child. In spite of all his efforts, he was left with only one viable conclusion: Sexual molestation was undetermined.

This much-respected pediatrician knew the court system, the time it took from his practice, the often disappointing results of failed litigation in the absence of physical findings and lack of verbal explanation by his young patients. He advised the grandmother of the absence of definitive findings, physical and otherwise, that would lead him to diagnose the child as molested. He advised her of additional symptoms to watch for and report, but concluded there was not enough data to warrant keeping the child from her mother and new stepfather. Three months later the child was re-examined and found to have vaginal bleeding and a broken hymen. The perpetrator was the mother's new mate. Ten years later, Dr. S. is still haunted by this case and his inability to intervene during the initial evaluation.

J.J. was a second-year medical student. He had seen a two-hour slide presentation during his freshman year on the developmental and psychological indicators of child sexual, physical and emotional abuse. He had been introduced to forms designed by Peterson and Hardin for the human figure drawing and kinetic family drawing assessment. It was an easy system. The child drew on one side of the paper and the clinician scored on the other side of the paper. Recently this medical student and his wife had been concerned about their four-year-old daughter, who quite suddenly displayed a fear of men, refused to go to her babysitter and engaged in frequent masturbation. Initially when he questioned his child she was reluctant to speak. He decided to have his daughter draw for him. Upon inspection of her human figure drawing, he found three art indicators of abuse. J.J. immediately took his daughter to a pediatrician trained in the assessment of child sexual abuse. It was determined by drawing analysis and child interview that his child was being fondled by her male adolescent babysitter. The quick identification of this molestation prevented any further trauma to this child, including penetration. The young perpetrator was reported and treated. There is a decade of difference between these two cases.

The book you hold in your hand is intended to assist you to identify early signs of child trauma communicated through drawings and interviews. You will find structured one-page screening tests for the human figure drawing (HFD) and kinetic family drawing (KFD). This art screening method can be compared with the structure provided by the Denver Developmental Screening Test, which organizes child developmental indicators on a single piece of paper for the medical file (Frankenburg, 1990). We believe child art productions should also be collected and filed in the overall evaluation of a child.

For those readers interested in the historical events that lead to the use and misuse of drawing interpretation, begin at the beginning with Chapter 1. For those readers primarily interested in implementing a clinical system of quantitative drawing assessment, begin with Chapter 2. For those who have an extensive background in quantitative approaches to art interpretation, turn to Chapter 3 (The Child Human Figure Drawing Inventory and Interview) and Chapter 4 (The Child Kinetic Family Drawing Inventory and Interview). One can review all of the child HFD and KFD drawings collected, in each chapter, and determine the criteria for scoring child art productions using this system. Finally one can review Appendix F to learn possible meanings of child art indicators. We encourage you to take the self-tests which appear at the end of both Chapter 3 (HFD) and Chapter 4 (KFD) before administering this screening instrument.

This book is intended for use by trained clinicians who are familiar with child assessment and interviews. Others using this screening inventory are encouraged to consult with a professional who has the appropriate training to interpret the findings. It is our hope that this work will extend your ability to see what cannot be heard when a child is emotionally distressed.

CHILDREN IN DISTRESS

A Guide for Screening
Children's Art

Chapter 1

Analysis and Interpretation of Children's Drawings

It is a basic human need to give expression to one's feelings and experiences—to give form to the unspeakable. Prehistoric man entered dark, remote caves and painted the walls and ceilings with images of fearful animals he encountered in the hunt. Egyptians and indigenous Americans drew in the tombs of their kings. What little is known about ancient African kingdoms comes by way of their art and pictographs. Out of the sight of guards in Nazi concentration camps, adults and children created art in secret. When asked why one would risk his life in order to draw, a survivor said, "We had to do it in order to live through each day" (Volavkova, 1978).

Children in modern society live in war and warlike situations of hostile divorce and custody battles, domestic violence, sexual, physical and emotional abuse. They endure invasive hospital procedures and devastating medical conditions. Much of the time they have neither the words nor the understanding to convey the pain and confusion of these frightening acts. Children experience victimization whether it is directed toward themselves or experienced vicariously through the lives of significant others (Terr, 1991). Often they are forced into silence out of fear of revealing family secrets or receiving retaliation. But they will draw. They will "tell without telling" their stories of fear and abuse through their art productions.

In every culture, whether with pen and paper or sticks in the sand, children draw. They draw what is important to them: people, shelter, trees and animals. They are spontaneous and less self-conscious than adults. Whereas speaking comes with difficulty, a child will draw what is direct and close to the truth.

Perceptually, children's art differs from that of adults in that children often disregard perspective and proportion. What has meaning is drawn largest and is most emphasized. In Terezin, Poland, the cook serving food is much larger than the people standing in line (Volavkova, 1978); in El Salvador, a wounded pregnant woman dominates in size and placement over soldiers and helicopters (Yornberger, 1986); in the modern hospital, a huge needle and syringe outsize the small person drawn in bed (H. Artman, personal communication, 1992); in an outpatient clinic, large male genitalia fill the page drawn by a child enduring sexual abuse (Peterson, 1990).

Children's art can also be less graphic and different in composition from that of adults. Children in stressful situations often draw what appears to be "gay" or "happy." A bright sun, a smiling face or a few bright flowers are added to a picture. Such qualities were observed in the 1980 and 1981 massacres of civilians in rural El Salvador (Yornberger, 1986). Children initially drew pictures of stark violence and bloodshed simulating their observations of the invasion. Later, the same children drew pictures of colorful vegetables growing in formerly blood-drenched soil.

When children insert these cheerful elements into their pictures are they showing us they can see hope and goodness in otherwise stressful situations? Or does drawing actually heal children? What if these "happy" components are a cover-up for unspeakable trauma, which if denoted more graphically would get a child in trouble?

In truth we don't know the exact meaning of these indicators. Any one or all of the above interpretations could apply to a specific child, a specific context or a specific time. We do know that cheerful elements exist in child art and that these qualities could deter the adult observer from taking the art seriously.

In Western culture, investigation into the meaning and analysis of children's drawings has taken place since the turn of the century. In spite of considerable research from a developmental and analytical perspective, clinicians continue to be criticized either for their overinterpretation or their inability to decipher and quantify children's drawings. Thus the child's primary method of communicating "secret subjects" remains undervalued by police, courts, social workers and health professionals. Yet these clinicians are the front-line "system," entrusted to provide child advocacy. Because the legal and medical community require objectivity and/or a scientific approach, this book presents a quanititative art analysis, so the child's expression on paper will be given more credence.

Case Example 1

On July 6, 1988, 4-year-old Heather M. died. An autopsy showed the cause of death to be a massive brain hemorrhage secondary to a blow to the head. There was also evidence consistent with other severe blows to the head as well as numerous, overlapping bruises on her buttocks. Heather had been physically abused and beaten to death. Her mother and stepfather were arrested and charged with murder (Reno Gazette-Journal, 1988).

Despite the fact that repeated complaints had been made to law enforcement and child welfare agencies for six months prior to her death, Heather was allowed to "slip through the cracks." This child showed a happy, smiling face to the people investigating her case. The most she would ever say was, "Mommy got mad because I was bad."

But Heather had been trying to tell someone what was happening to her. She left cries for help scribbled in grotesque faces drawn with crayon and ink in the closet of her bedroom. After her death, these pictures were discovered by the couple who moved into her parents' vacated trailer. These drawings were different from the one collected by Dr. S. from Susan. There was no evidence of genitalia, but faces were drawn in red ink with tiny crosses for eyes and down-turned, jagged mouths. Not a happy face, but the face of a desperate, physically abused child, afraid and unable to communicate in any other way. If professionals had discovered these drawings and known how to interpret them, would Heather's life have had a different outcome?

Purpose of this Manual

This manual attempts to fill the need for a reliable and practical screening tool for child art productions that incorporates both the quantitative and qualitative aspects of a drawing. Although many books exist on children's art, professionals need an up-to-date scoring system that includes a look at both the individual child and the child within the family.

Children in Distress takes the reader through a step-by-step procedure so the clinician can be self-taught in a period of two to three hours. Self-tests and figures with descriptions are incorporated for self-learning. The art indicators have been redrawn by a professional artist from actual child drawings. This unique feature provides consistency so the reader can focus on learning the specific indicator without the complexity of a variety of formats from child line drawings. A one-page scoring form permits the child to draw on one side and the clinician to score on the other side.

The clinician is taught how to set up and retrieve drawings in the practice setting. Scoring guides are included for both the human figure drawing (HFD) and kinetic family drawing (KFD), which will be described later in the manual. The child is requested to either "Draw a picture of a person using just your pencil, a whole person, not a stick figure—the best person you can draw" or "Draw a picture of everyone in your family, including you, DOING something. Try to draw whole people, not cartoons or stick people" (Burns & Kaufman, 1972). Once the drawing is complete, the practitioner turns the paper over and scores the indicators, making the work suitable for placement in a child's medical, school or legal file. Follow-up interview guides are available when the score results in a suspicion of emotional distress.

Why Use Child Art Productions?

Clinicians caring for children are continually searching for assessment tools to easily and effectively ascertain a child's developmental and emotional status. Many assessment tools used by clinicians depend heavily upon sophisticated verbalizations (such as the Children's Apperception Test and Divorce Story Telling Cards), yet children are still developing language abilities. The language abilities a child may possess can be severely challenged in trying to relate to adults an emotional trauma that has recently been experienced. Alternative methods of assessment need to be utilized to encourage children's nonverbal communications. Any method that may assist the clinician to investigate and validate the child's emotional and developmental status warrants consideration.

The use of art for screening purposes has several distinct advantages for clinicians:

- Children are more likely to engage in art activity, which allows for a self-directed, gradual relating of their experience, than in a time-urgent adult interview.
- There is growing literature documenting an unconscious need for children to re-enact the trauma they have experienced (Terr, 1981, 1983). Re-enactment in the form of art and play is healthy and positive.

- Art allows for tension release, as the child's mental energy is redirected from dealing with strong emotions to focusing on the artistic expression of emotions.
- This redirection enables the child to attain new perspectives and insights into his trauma.
- The child's art production can later be shared with others who have experienced the same situation.

Children's drawings represent an intervention that is easily implemented, at minimal cost, in a school, hospital or health care setting where traumatized children are being treated (Peterson, 1990).

A Message to the Clinician

Priority

Victimization of children, especially through physical, emotional or sexual abuse, has received increasing attention from professionals and the media in recent years. Studies of adults in the United States have found that l in 3 girls and 1 in 5 boys were victims of sexual abuse as children (Ards & Harrell, 1993; Feldman, Feldman, Goodman, & McGrath, 1991; Finkelhor & Dziuba-Leatherman, 1994; VanderMey, 1988; Vandeven & Emans, 1992; Waterman, Kelley, Oliveri, & McCord, 1993). Current research confirms a tripling in the incidence of reported child sexual abuse since 1980 (Finkelhor & Dziuba-Leatherman, 1994; Kessler & Hyden, 1991; Spencer & Dunklee, 1986; Wilkins, 1990). As adults and teenagers come forward and speak of their abuse, clinicians are becoming more aware of the devastation caused by this problem (Martin, Anderson, Romans, Mullen, & O'Shea, 1993). Several studies during the last decade have generally confirmed the earlier research, which claimed a multitude of negative emotional and behavioral effects for both male and female victims of child sexual molestation (Burgess, Hartman, McCausland, & Powers, 1984; Everstein & Everstein, 1989; Faller, 1984; Kempe & Kempe, 1984; Leaman, 1980; Sgroi, 1982; Summit, 1983).

The negative emotional consequences most commonly reported are fear, anxiety, depression, anger and hostility, in varying degrees of severity (MacFarland & Waterman, 1986; Sgroi, 1982). The negative behavioral consequences that have been identified include aggression, self-destructive tendencies and inappropriate re-enactment of the very behavior that was perpetrated upon the child (Browne & Finkelhor, 1986; De Francis, 1969; Meiselman, 1978; Peters, 1976; Terr, 1991). Regardless of which negative effects a child may experience as a result of victimization by an adult, the effects are severe and longstanding unless they are promptly identified and treated. Early intervention with this group of children can help prevent future psychopathology.

Position

Clinicians in medical settings, schools and the legal system are in optimal positions to intervene with children who have been victimized. These clinicians have early and frequent access to children as well as the means to initiate change during crises. Children who have been victimized commonly present with changes in behavior or unexplained trauma at routine physical/developmental checkups or changes in school performance. Front-line clinicians underdetect children suffering from abuse and need tools and training to identify these children. In a study conducted in Finister, France, asking family practice, obstetric, pediatric and general physicians to determine a diagnosis of 1500 children known to be sexually abused, only 64 were correctly identified (Baccino et al., 1995). Physical symptoms were often not evident in these children and they were reluctant to reveal their abuse. Van der Kolk (1988, 1994) has recently reported that the brain encodes sensorimotor and auditory trauma stimuli (not cognitive/linguistic stimuli) up to the age of four years. One might theorize that young children are therefore more able to reveal their trauma through re-enactment play and drawing than through verbal means. The clinician who retrieves and documents child art over time in medical/school records may have an aid to early detection.

Practice

Although drawing interpretation has largely been done by psychologists, these practitioners are often second in line to evaluate child trauma, after referral from other child care professionals. Considerable research into child art has already been undertaken by physicians who recognize the value of art communication in enhancing interaction with children (Baldwin, 1964; Burns & Kaufman, 1972; Coles, 1992; DiLeo, 1983; Miller, 1981).

While the practitioner of medicine, education or counseling may exclaim, "I don't even know where to start to screen child art," many of the skills essential to this approach are already in the repertoire of the practitioner. The physician knows how to survey the body cephalocaudally, to determine deviation from the norm, to identify symmetry and to discern fine detail of physical abnormality. The teacher makes an overall appraisal of a child, including his or her appearance, on-task behavior, sensory learning styles and academic performance. The family counselor knows how to look at family systems, positions and perceived power. These cognitive mind sets are identical to the skills needed to analyze a child's art work. The physician will find the enclosed scoring forms similar in structure to the Denver Developmental Screening Test (DDST) (Frankenburg, Dodds, & Fandal, 1973). The teacher will find that the drawing screening forms enhance the overall individual educational program (IEP). The marriage and family counselor will have tangible evidence of child perceptions of the family.

Clinicians bring a wealth of ability to this task, which requires a holistic as well as detailed discrimination of unique art indicators.

Reliability and Validity in Drawing Interpretation

In order to give credence to the use of drawings in clinical practice, a method must exist for determining whether a child's drawing interpretation stands the test of reliability and validity. Reliability in a drawing method means that similar findings are reproduced with different children under similar circumstances. Inter-rater reliability means that two raters would look at the same drawing, score it and come to similar conclusions. Validity in a drawing refers to whether the identified aspects in a person's drawing really indicate potential pathology or health. Additionally, the scoring of child art must be quantifiable so that many raters would come to the same conclusion after scoring a single art production.

Premises of Drawing Methodology and Interpretation

Two major systems have evolved in child art interpretation based on very different premises. One is based on a qualitative, projective analysis; the other is based on a quantitative appraisal (present or absent indicators) in a child's drawing. Research has traditionally focused primarily on human figure drawings (HFDs) but more recently kinetic family drawings (KFDs) produced by a child have also been addressed. The HFD is generally considered the child's representation of the self; the KFD shows the child's perception of the interpersonal relationships and support among family members.

Qualitative Analysis

Qualitative analysis stems from the work of Buck (1948a) and Machover (1949). Their use of HFDs to uncover psychological and emotional information is one of the oldest and most controversial of all associative techniques (Palmer, 1983; Sundbert, 1961). The rationale is that children's HFDs divulge the extent to which the child has developed some image of his own body and the physical aspects of others (Machover, 1955; Palmer, 1983). The qualitative hypothesis presumes that the "self" is projected into the drawings of the human figure by the artist. Interpretation is based on this direct analogy. Machover (1953) is most closely identified with projective techniques. She states that the HFD relates intimately to the impulses, anxieties, conflicts and compensations characteristic of the individual producing the HFD (Buck, 1948b; Machover, 1953, 1955, 1960). Her method considers how well the drawing is composed, including the formal structure, placement and pressure of the pencil. In particular, Machover emphasizes body parts, including size, shape, position and erasures.

Modifications of the Machover method include the house-tree-person (H-T-P) test by Buck (1948a, 1948b). The H-T-P was designed to yield information about the child's perception and interaction with his environment, maturity, sensitivity and personality integration. The use of children's HFDs as projective tools, expressions of their unconscious projections, is also associated with the work of Freud and Jung who considered art next to dreams as a pathway into the unconscious (Levy, 1958). Others have supported this view (Altschuler & Hattwick, 1947; Bell, 1948; Buck, 1948a, 1948b).

Another qualitative method involved the use of the KFD. Developed by Burns and Kaufman (1970), the emphasis in this method is on interpreting the actions, styles and symbols within the drawing to assess disturbances in the family system. Finally, regressed kinetic family drawings (RKFD) were developed by Furth (1988); in these an adult is requested to draw himself and his family at the age of five years. This can yield some of the significant themes of a person's life when compared to a drawing of the family as perceived at the present. This work has been replicated with medical students who drew their early family life experience and assessed how it affected their performance with children in clinical situations (Peterson & Rahe, 1991).

Koppitz (1984) suggested that there are four different projective uses for children's HFDs: as a measure of personality (Buck, 1948a, 1948b; Machover, 1949); as a measure of self in relation to others (Burns & Kaufman, 1970); as a measure of group values (Dennis, 1964); and as a measure of attitudes (Hammer, 1960).

Note the picture drawn by an eighth-grade boy depicting his doctor in Figure 1. The qualitative analysis by Klepsch and Logie (1982) was, "The doctor gives up on others (and himself?)."

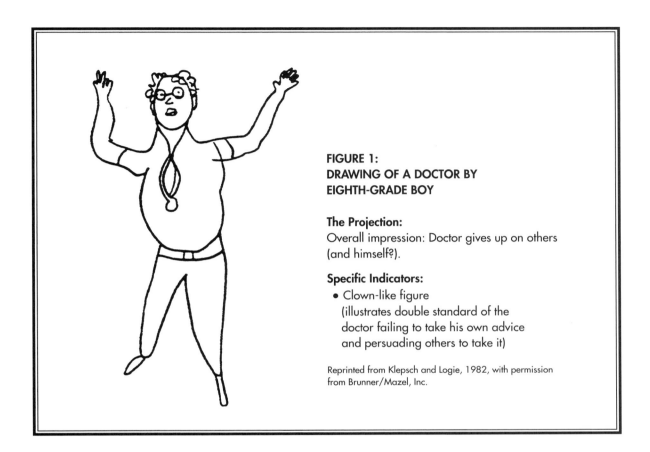

**FIGURE 1:
DRAWING OF A DOCTOR BY
EIGHTH-GRADE BOY**

The Projection:
Overall impression: Doctor gives up on others (and himself?).

Specific Indicators:
• Clown-like figure
(illustrates double standard of the doctor failing to take his own advice and persuading others to take it)

Reprinted from Klepsch and Logie, 1982, with permission from Brunner/Mazel, Inc.

The interpreters postulated that, "The clown-like figure illustrates the double standard of the doctor failing to take his own advice and persuading others to take it."

Criticism has come from members of the medical and forensic community who state that there is not much evidence to support such interpretations. And in fact we believe it is precisely this type of interpretation that has diminished the credibility of child drawings as a source of information for legal or medical use (Cox, 1993).

Using the Hardin/Peterson HFD quantitative analysis would result in a score of this drawing as normal. The analysis of "the doctor giving up on himself and others" would be unwarranted.

Quantitative Analysis

Quantitative analysis was first developed through the research of Goodenough (1926, 1928) and Harris (1963), who correlated the HFD with intellectual ability. Their scoring systems were founded on the developmental levels and general intellectual abilities exhibited in a large sample of children's drawings. A table was devised to show the relative frequency of certain characteristics in the drawings of normal boys and girls at various ages. These approaches standardized

FIGURE 2: ASSESSING DEVELOPMENTAL LEVELS OF DRAWING

APPROX. AGE (YRS.)	DESCRIPTION OF DRAWING	CHARACTERISTIC DRAWINGS
0-1	The infant has a reflex response to visual stimuli. The crayon is brought to the mouth but the infant does not draw.	
1-2	At approximately 13 months, the first scribble appears: a zig-zag. The infant watches the movement of the crayon leaving its marks on the surface.	
2-4	Circles appear and gradually predominate. The circles then become discrete. In a casually drawn circle, the child envisages an object. A first graphic symbol has been made, usually between 3 and 4 years old.	
4-7	In this stage of intellectual realism, the child draws an internal model, not what is actually seen. The child draws what is known to be there. Transparencies, such as showing people through walls and hulls of ships, are commonly produced. Drawings at this age are expressionistic and subjective.	
7-12	During this stage of visual realism, subjectivity diminishes. The child draws what is actually visible. Human figures are more realistic and proportioned. Colors are more conventional. The child distinguishes the right from the left side of the figure drawn.	
12+	With the development of the critical faculty, most children lose interest in drawing. The gifted tend to persevere.	

Data from DiLeo, 1983.

the way children were instructed to draw and laid the groundwork for all subsequent techniques of drawing methodology and interpretation.

DiLeo (1970, 1983) also documented normal developmental stages in child art. Figure 2 shows the developmental progression of a child's art from birth to adolescence. The child from birth to 3 years scribbles spontaneously; from 3–4 years the child draws a three-part man with extremities coming from the head. This kind of figure was noted by Ricci (1887) and called cephalopods or tadpole figures. Cox (1993) reported that in a sample of 133 tadpole-drawers, the ages range from 2 years 11 months to 6 years 2 months with a mean age of 4 years 1 month. The incorporation of the torso by age 5–6 is a critical milestone and is the main criterion for the conventional human figure drawing (Cox & Parkin, 1986). According to Gesell (1925), 67% of children age 5–7 years draw a six-part man with extremities coming from the body. With age, children do not continue to use single lines for the limbs. By age 6, most children draw double lines to represent limbs (Koppitz, 1968; Papadakis-Michaelides, 1989). By 7–9 years they attempt to draw in profile. By 10-13 years they produce objective body representations (Goodenough, 1926; Harris, 1963; Koppitz, 1968). After 13 years of age, children become more interested in drawing portraits than whole figures (Cox, 1993).

Interestingly, ears and a neck rarely appear in children's HFDs prior to the age of 5, but feet/shoes are commonly included in drawings by the same age group (Cox, 1993).

Children and adults often regress in stressful situations. Thus, one might use a developmental perspective to examine the discrepancy between expected and actual art ability at a chronological stage to determine the level of regression in a traumatized child.

Detection of Emotional Abuse Indicators in Drawings

Koppitz (1966a, 1966b, 1967, 1968, 1984) refined the Goodenough scoring system and applied it to children with emotional and psychological problems (see Appendix A). She quantified various indicators. First, the quality of the overall drawing was noted: shading, symmetry, size, shape, slant and transparency. Second, spontaneously added items or unusual components (e.g., teeth, genitals, big hands, clouds) were evaluated. Third, omissions of items that would typically be expected on the HFDs of children at a given age (e.g., eyes, nose, mouth, body, arms, legs, feet, neck) were scored. Thirty emotional indicators appeared more often in the drawings of children identified with unsatisfactory interpersonal relationships and emotional problems than in the drawings of normal children. In a matched group of 76 well-adjusted children (ages 5–12) and 76 children in a child guidance clinic (ages 5–12), the normal children produced 22 emotional indicators, whereas the clinic population produced 166. Furthermore, 58 of the 76 well-adjusted children drew no indicators at all (refer to Table 1).

Koppitz (1968) went on to compare children rated as aggressive (n=31) to shy (n=31), noting that the aggressive children drew more indicators than the shy children (90 compared to 75). Indicators drawn by aggressive children included asymmetry of limbs, teeth, long arms, big hands and cut-off hands. The shy children more often omitted the mouth. When Cox (1993) reanalyzed these data, she confirmed that the Koppitz indicators differentiated shy from aggressive children except that no significant differences were noted in the presence of big hands or the omission of the mouth.

The validity of the Koppitz scoring system has been tested by several investigators who concluded that emotional indicators occur more often in HFDs of disturbed children. Thus over

---

TABLE 1: THE 30 EMOTIONAL ITEMS IN KOPPITZ'S DRAW-A-PERSON TEST

1. Poor integration of parts
2. Shading of face
3. Shading of body and/or limbs
4. Shading of hands and/or neck
5. Gross asymmetry of limbs
6. Slanting figure
7. Tiny figure
8. Big figure
9. Transparencies
10. Tiny head
11. Crossed eyes
12. Teeth
13. Short arms
14. Long arms
15. Arms clinging to body
16. Big hands
17. Hands cut off
18. Legs pressed together
19. Genitals
20. Monster or grotesque figure
21. 3 or more figures spontaneous
22. Clouds
23. No eyes
24. No nose
25. No mouth
26. No body
27. No arms
28. No legs
29. No feet
30. No neck

Data from Koppitz, 1968

---

time the Koppitz system has become the standard for quantitative interpretation. In order to qualify as an indicator, the following criteria must be met (Koppitz, 1966a, 1966b, 1966c):

- The indicator must have clinical validity, i.e., it must be able to differentiate between HFDs of children with and without emotional problems.
- The indicator must be unusual and occur infrequently on the HFDs of normal children, i.e., the sign must be present in less than 16 percent of the HFDs of children at a given age level.
- The indicator must not be related to age or maturation, i.e., its frequency of occurrence on HFDs must not increase solely on the basis of increase in age.

In this system an indicator is scored as either present or absent and no interpretation is made. In scoring the aforementioned picture of the doctor (Figure 1), the quantitative analysis would find no emotional indicators. Quantification permits two or more observers to come to the same conclusion regarding a child's drawing.

Detection of Sexual Abuse Indicators in Drawings

There is a paucity of literature on the HFDs of sexually molested children. Goodwin (1982) concluded that drawings are helpful in evaluating incest victims under the age of 12, but by themselves are not sufficient to make a diagnostic decision. Yates, Beutler, and Crago (1985) found that child victims of incest had poorly developed impulse control and were more variable in the expression of sexual features in their drawings than non-abused children. Kaufman and Wohl (1992) provided a developmental perspective for sexual abuse using projective drawings.

Using the criteria developed by Koppitz, Hardin (1989) attempted to identify indicators that differentiate sexually abused children (ages 6–10 years) from emotionally impaired and normal children (ages 6–10 years). Hardin looked at a total of 842 children's HFDs from three different groups (see Appendix B). The first group was 341 children who had been positively identified as sexually molested. The second group comprised 252 clinic-referred children with emotional or behavioral problems. This group had been professionally determined not to have been sexually molested. The third group of 249 children were from the general population grades K–4, ages 6–10 years. The K–4 population was not prescreened for sexual or emotional problems, but none had been identified as molested or emotionally distressed.

In the Hardin study, the number and type of sexual indicators (SIs) present in the three groups of children's HFDs were examined. Seven of the SIs appeared significantly more often in the HFDs of the sexually molested children than in those of the other children: explicit drawing of genitals, concealment of genitals, omission of genital region, omission of central part of figure, encapsulation, fruit trees added and opposite sex from the artist drawn (see Table 2). The presence of even one of these indicators should alert the clinician that sexual molestation is possible and a carefully focused physical exam and interview are warranted (Hardin, 1989).

TABLE 2: "SERIOUS SEVEN" INDICATORS FOR SCREENING CHILDREN'S DRAWINGS

Explicit drawing of genitals
Concealment of genitals
Omission of genital region
Omission of central part of figure
Encapsulation of drawing
Fruit trees added
Opposite sex drawn

Data from Hardin, 1989

Although one might think that the presence of genitalia in a picture is related to nudity in the home, access to sexually explicit materials or sexual education, Hibbard and Foghmann (1987) determined that such practices were not associated with Western child drawings of genitalia.

In the Hardin study, some of the original Koppitz emotional indicators were coded differently. For example, Koppitz's third indicator, "shading of body and/or limbs," and her fourth indicator, "shading of hands and/or neck," were both coded in the Hardin study as "shading—body." Furthermore, "legs pressed together" by Koppitz was coded as "legs tightly together" by Hardin (see Appendix C).

Six traditional Koppitz emotional indicators were included but did not significantly differentiate the sexually molested group from the other two groups when a factor analysis was done. Some Koppitz indicators, while not statistically significant, did represent a trend which may be clinically important. The clinical indicator "legs tightly together" occurred in 12.3% of the molested children, 8.3% of the clinic-referred children and 10% of the general population. The clinical indicator "hands cut off" occurred in 26.7% of the HFDs of the molested children, 24.6% of the clinic-referred children and 13.7% of the general population. Note that the general population was not screened for the presence of sexually molested children (see Appendix B, page 130). In the Hardin study, some Koppitz indicators occurred more frequently in the non-molested groups. As an example, the indicator "transparencies" occurred in 12.3% of the HFDs of molested children versus 47.2% of the HFDs of the other groups. "Tiny figure" occurred in 4.7% of the HFDs of molested children, 55.2% of the clinic-referred children and 30% of the general population. In the Hardin study, there were no significant differences among the three groups with regard to the clinical indicators "slanting figure" and "big hands." The percentages of the Hardin sexual indicators in the three groups, including the emotional indicators selected from the work of Koppitz, are given in Appendix D. The Hardin/Peterson HFD inventory (page 40), was organized to present the most-to-least serious of sexual and emotional indicators for detecting traumatized children. A quantitative score of 3–5 or 6+ is required before a child interview or referral is recommended. The inventory is intended as a broad screening tool for potential emotional, sexual or physical indicators which a child may communicate through drawing. Even though some indicators were not highly discriminative in the Hardin study, they have been included in the HFD inventory when the authors deemed they were widely used by Koppitz and other professionals.

Detection of Physical Abuse Indicators in Drawings

The authors know of no large quantitative study (similar to that of Hardin) that has focused on the art indicators of physically abused children. DiLeo (1973, 1977) identified several indicators from his clinical practice seen in the art work of the physically/emotionally abused child. These included scattered body parts, grotesque, bizarre figures, scribbling over a drawn figure, excessive shading and rigid, robot-like figures. Qualitative interpretations of art work by children from violent homes has been comprehensively covered by Wohl and Kaufman (1985). The Hardin/Peterson quantitative HFD inventory includes the DiLeo indicators and identifies other indicators of the physically abused noted in the authors' clinical practices (e.g., jagged teeth and Xs for eyes). More quantitative drawing research is needed for this clinical population.

Kinetic Family Drawings

The first presentation of the technique in which children were requested to draw "a family" or "their family" was introduced by Hulse (1951), who hypothesized that drawings provide clues to intrafamilial conflict. Burns and Kaufman (1970) incorporated this idea and requested further that the child draw a picture of the family "doing something." These renderings were called *kinetic* family drawings. When the child draws the family "doing something," more information can be retrieved about the child's perception of family members' interaction or isolation. The emphasis in analyzing the KFD is on interpreting actions, styles and symbols in the drawing to assess the presence or absence of perceived support from the family system.

DiLeo (1973) distinguishes the HFD from the KFD by emphasizing the difference in the cognitive/affective ratio. He maintains that the HFD is predominantly the expression of one's cognitive ability, whereas the KFD requires the mobilization of feelings toward those one regards as most important. He notes that KFD figures taken separately are frequently an inferior product to the HFD produced alone, due to the expression of emotional material.

Most young children draw convergent pictures of the family members standing in a line facing forward. Importance is expressed by size, with the most important person drawn largest and the least powerful drawn smallest. Affinity is symbolically expressed by closeness to the artist or similarity in attire, whereas child rejection results in delegation of a person to the edge of the paper or elimination of the person.

Older children are able to portray movement and can depict family members in profile as well as full face. The clinician looks for mood, physical proximity, interactions, body parts and style of drawing, including encapsulation, isolation, barriers or extensions drawn between members. Burns and Kaufman (1972) comprehensively examined the symbology of these actions and relations. In a study conducted by Meyers (1978), 116 boys were evaluated using the KFD form to distinguish emotionally healthy from emotionally disturbed children. The results of Meyers's study showed the variables listed above to differentiate these two groups. The variables that make up the KFD scoring system have shown high interrater reliability. In a study by Mostkoff and Lazarus (1983), test-retest reliabilities ranged from 46% to 90%. The reliability of omission of body parts, slanting figures, arm extensions, elevated figures, barriers and drawings on the back of the page ranged from 70% to 90%.

It is well-known that one's perception of self within the network of the family has considerable impact on one's response to treatment. The use of KFDs has elicited the closeness or isolation experienced by diabetic children within a family system (Sayed & Leaverton, 1974); elucidated a child's response to eye surgery and his perception of his family's disapproval (Steiner & Peterson, 1992); and shown the response of bereaved children who place the deceased on the baseline with other family members prior to treatment and show the deceased floating above baseline when bereavement issues are resolved (Peterson, Nitsch, & Higgins, 1994).

Before turning to the use of the HFD and KFD inventories, three other factors need to be addressed in order for one's drawing interpretation to be valid and accepted in the professional arena: the number of indicators, cultural differences and context. Finally, the art inventory is one tool in the overall appraisal of a child, which includes an interview of the child alone, a child physical exam and follow-up investigation (e.g., with peers, school officials, neighbors, relatives).

Frequency of Indicators and Cultural Differences

Koppitz (1968, 1984) and DiLeo (1983) emphasize the importance of assessing the child according to the total number of emotional indicators. One should never make a diagnosis on the basis of one single indicator because of the different ways children may express the same indicator.

In addition, Koppitz (1968) suggested that age and social and cultural background be evaluated. Court (1989) showed that the same criteria are not applicable to all cultures. Whereas most Western children include eyes in their drawings of facial features, African children frequently omit the eyes. Fortes (1940, 1981) studied the Tallensi in the Northern Territories of the Gold Coast, and found they had no two-dimensional art representations. The Tallensi children (ages 6–16) were able to sculpt small human figures, but drew stick figures with a small head like a stick pin and no facial features.

Genitalia are usually omitted in the drawings of non-abused children in Western culture, but are frequently and accurately incorporated in cultures such as the Tallensi. Any attempts to take a scoring system based on data from one culture/society and apply it to another would be scientifically invalid.

Contextual Considerations in Drawing Interpretation

The context in which a drawing is produced can affect one's interpretation of that drawing. Spontaneous drawings are usually produced by a child with no special instructions and brought to the clinician by the parents. Instructed drawings are those produced following instructions by the clinician in a controlled setting with the client fully conscious. Another form of instructed drawings occurs when the person is in an altered state, for example, during relaxation and imagery. Achterberg (1985; Achterberg & Lawlis, 1984) relaxed cancer patients and asked them to visualize their white blood cells, cancer cells and treatment modality (chemotherapy or radiation). Using criteria based on size, activity and vividness, she was able to tell with 80% accuracy the likelihood of patients surviving (personal communication, 1993). After drawing, her patients were interviewed. She then combined the images from the drawing with the patient interview and quantified the patient's response to treatment. In these cases, drawing related to self-imagery was an "aid" to understanding the patient's expectation of outcome.

Directed drawings are usually produced by a child who has been given specific instructions to reproduce someone or something in his or her environment. An art therapist might ask a child to draw the perpetrator or molestation scene. When a child is instructed to "show everyone in your family doing something," the drawing would be classified as directed.

This manual seeks to incorporate both the individual drawing of the self and the drawing of the family using a quantitative approach to provide insight into the child's self and family system. As with Achterberg's work, this approach to child art utilizes follow-up interview guides. The scoring forms are to be used with the child fully conscious in the controlled environment of the clinician's office.

Organization and Use of this Manual

Several drawing methods and scoring systems have been discussed thus far. They are listed in Table 3.

TABLE 3: QUALITATIVE AND QUANTITATIVE ANALYSIS	
QUALITATIVE ANALYSIS (Interpretive)	**QUANTITATIVE ANALYSIS** (Scoring Systems)
1. Machover (1949, 1953)	1. Koppitz (1968, 1984)
2. DiLeo (1973, 1983)	2. Vane and Eisen (1962)
3. Buck (1948a, 1948b)	3. Dillard and Landsman (1968)
4. Hammer (1960)	4. Burns and Kaufman (1972)
5. Jolles (1971)	5. Peterson and Hardin (1995)

Some of these systems have had limited use in medical and school systems because of complexity of administration or interpretation. Clinicians need time-efficient methods that do not require highly complex techniques. Furthermore, there is controversy among investigators about the meaning of various indicators. One author might regard clouds in a child's drawing to mean "feeling gloomy," whereas another would contend the child has a "dark cloud over his head." Although anyone can postulate meaning, there is no way to give an exact meaning to each individual drawing. Based on statistical analysis, it is known that emotionally disturbed children treat drawings differently from non-disturbed children. Thus, their indicators are a red flag for further investigation. (Turn to Appendices E and H to identify commonly held meanings for the HFD and KFD indicators.)

Using the screening inventories in this manual should result in the ability:

- to assess the developmental stage of a child's drawing.
- to detect psychological or emotional drawing indicators.
- to detect unspoken victimization (i.e., sexual, emotional or physical abuse).
- to assess family dynamics (the child's perception of self and others within the family system).

The following case documents how all four of these objectives can be met in the interpretation of a child's drawing within a routine clinical practice.

Case Example 2

Jane, age 4, was seen by a pediatrician for personality changes, behavior problems and frequent nightmares. She had physical findings of labial erythema, abrasions and vaginal bleeding, suggesting sexual abuse. The child was unresponsive to interview or the use of anatomically correct dolls to disclose her victimization. She would not give any information as to what had taken place except to say that she "rubbed" herself. After leaving the office that day she told her mother that she had "lied to the lady."

Some days later, Jane's mother noted the child's excoriated labia and discharge again while bathing her. Upon her second visit to the office, the mother said that her daughter had mentioned "magic spoons," but would give no further information. The clinician (L.W.P., author) attempted puppet play without success. She then gave Jane paper and pencils and said, "Draw me a picture of a person." This worked. Jane drew, and eventually discussed what had happened. She initially drew two large phallic symbols (long cylindrical, cigar-shaped torsos). As if she had an afterthought, she quickly turned the paper and drew faces on each, to disguise what she had revealed (Figure 3).

The clinician said, "Tell me more about your drawing" and made verbatim notes of the child's words. Pointing to the two phallic symbols, the child said, "These are the magic spoons."

Some direct but not leading questions were asked of Jane. These questions were posed to the child as a choice of a pair of ideas such as "Was it daytime or nighttime?" and "Is the magic spoon older or younger than you?" She replied, "They are older." Jane was asked, "What do you do with the magic spoon?" She replied, "It lays on me." At this point Jane was asked, "Can I write on your paper?" The child nodded, and the clinician wrote the child's pertinent quotes in anticipation of future forensic study.

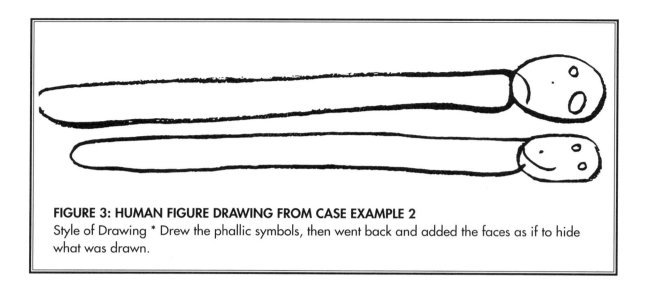

FIGURE 3: HUMAN FIGURE DRAWING FROM CASE EXAMPLE 2
Style of Drawing * Drew the phallic symbols, then went back and added the faces as if to hide what was drawn.

Once Jane revealed this information from the HFD, she was asked to "draw your family, including yourself, doing something" (kinetic family drawing). The symmetry between family members was noted to show no unusual indicators (Figure 4). The family drawing was also developmentally normal for a 4-year-old, who will usually draw the extremities coming out of the head. Jane was also asked to draw a picture of her grandparents (Figure 5). This drawing was also normal. In order to determine where Jane's abuse might be occurring, the child was asked to draw the important people at the babysitter's. The first two figures were drawn in keeping with her former style, but the last two figures were drawn with a completely different style of mouth (Figure 6). This change in symmetry can be an important clue to the child's communications. While drawing these last two forms, Jane spontaneously said, "They told me about magic spoons." The investigator asked, "Do these spoons have names?"

"Yes."

Jane was then encouraged to leave her drawing and go to the dollhouse. She picked up two small dolls. She put a girl doll in bed and put two boy dolls on top of her. She said, "They would hurt her . . . that would hurt too . . . the tummy would get red." In this case, the drawing led to the revelation that two teenaged boys molested Jane while at the babysitter's house.

This case is presented to illustrate several points. First, the presentation of a child in trouble is usually not just physically based, but often includes emotional findings. Second, the usual method of interviewing will not always work with a young child. Even role-playing with dolls or puppets may not reveal the truth. But the drawing method can open the line of communication for the child to reveal what has happened. Finally, the drawings also provide an indelible impression that can be shared with other clinicians.

To achieve the objectives of this manual, the clinician is advised to adapt a systematic approach to the administration and interpretation of children's art. The screening inventory for

FIGURE 4:
KINETIC FAMILY DRAWING FROM CASE EXAMPLE 2

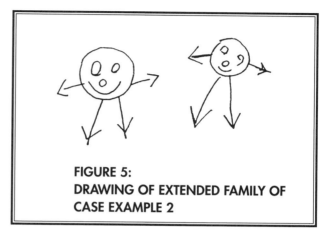

FIGURE 5:
DRAWING OF EXTENDED FAMILY OF CASE EXAMPLE 2

FIGURE 6:
DRAWING OF PEOPLE AT THE BABY-SITTER'S BY CHILD OF CASE EXAMPLE 2
Child Dialogue: "They told me about magic spoons."

child human figure drawing (page 40) is strictly quantitative, based on the research of Koppitz (1966a, 1966b, 1966c, 1968) and Hardin (1989). The Koppitz research is presented in Appendix A. The Hardin human figure drawing research is contained in Appendix B. Appendix C compares the Koppitz and Hardin indicators. The data and context of the Hardin study are presented in Appendix D. The screening inventory for kinetic family drawing (page 64) is based on the work of Burns & Kaufman (1970, 1972), but is reorganized for ease of scoring into a system that utilizes both quantitative and qualitative measures. The specifics of working with this system are elaborated in Chapters 2, 3 and 4.

Chapter 2

Implementing the Drawing Method

Supplies and Setting

- Establish the atmosphere in which the drawing can be performed so the child cannot imitate the work of others or feel that he or she is being scrutinized. An open, semi-private area allows the child to draw without too many distractions. The environment should be clear of other child drawings. If more than one child is drawing, space should be provided between them to avoid imitation.

- Provide a large selection of no. 2 pencils for the most realistic interpretation. Colored pencils are optional and compelling to children. The clinician must be aware that the quantitative interpretation of color has no current research base. Avoid the use of markers or crayons because they do not allow for the detail needed for drawing interpretation. Include an eraser, so the child can make changes. The paper should be white and at least 8½" x 11". Include a protractor for the evaluator, not the child, to measure for "tiny figure" (less than 3" on an 8½" x 11" piece of paper) and slant (15° from vertical).

- Parents, siblings and other persons significant to the child should not be left alone with the child as he or she draws. The child should not be watched by family or friends, or interrupted or questioned at any time about the art production. Once the drawing is complete, the child should not be asked, "Why did you/did you not include . . ." or "What does . . . mean?"

- Supply a hospitalized patient with a board in order to draw in bed.

Instructions

Human Figure Drawing

I would like you to draw me a picture of a person using just your pencil. I would like the drawing to be a whole person, not a stick figure—the best person you can draw.

Keep in mind that the HFD is the most difficult to draw and will require encouragement from the examiner. A child will often say, "Should I draw a lady or a man?" Respond with, "It's your drawing, draw whatever person you want to make." Some will say, "I don't know how to draw." Respond with, "Don't worry about making it perfect, I'm not judging your drawing skills."

Kinetic Family Drawing

Draw a picture of everyone in your family, including you, DOING something. Try to draw whole people, not cartoons or stick people. Remember, make everyone DOING something—some kind of action. (Burns & Kaufman, 1972).

The child may or may not label persons with names, and upon picture completion it is important to ask the child for this information.

Labeling

When you look at the completed drawing, be sure to ask the child for the age, name and sex of each person in the picture. Ask his or her permission to write this information under each figure or at the bottom of the page. Direct quotes by the child are added at the bottom of the form under Notes. Your clinical observations are also noted here, for example, "Child drew quickly" or "Child drew with heavy lining on the page." Avoid writing what you think this means. For example, instead of writing "Child was angry," write "Tightened his jaw, engaged in deep breathing." Write what you *see* him doing, not what you think his behavior *means.*

Table 4 summarizes the implementation of the drawing method.

Overinterpretation

Interpretation of Personality

It is essential to avoid making global statements about the personality of the child from one drawing. It is also important not to project the personality of the interpreter into the work of the artist. Much criticism of qualitative interpretation involves the use of the drawing as a method of explaining the child's perception (i.e., putting meaning into the work). The earlier example (Figure 1) of the eighth-grade boy who drew a picture of his doctor exemplified this when it was postulated that the "doctor gives up on others (and himself?)." Swenson (1968) and Cox (1993) have criticized these interpretations for lack of evidence.

Overinterpretation from One Drawing

It is not possible to diagnose psychological illness in a child from the indicators present in a single drawing. Under no circumstances can conclusions be drawn from the presence of only one indicator. Two or more indicators, especially those noted as the "serious seven" (see Table 2, page 25) and the screening inventory (page 40), warrant the clinician's immediate attention. Areas of concern for further investigation are identified by attending to the drawing as a whole. Sequential drawings may provide additional information and can also be used to assess progress during healing.

TABLE 4: SUGGESTIONS FOR IMPLEMENTING THE DRAWING METHOD

SUPPLIES

- Pencils
- Erasers
- Protractor (for evaluator)
- 8½" x 11" white paper

INSTRUCTIONS

Human Figure Drawing

"I would like you to draw me a picture of a person using just your pencil. I would like the drawing to be a whole person, not a stick figure—the best person you can draw."

Kinetic Family Drawing

"Draw a picture of everyone in your family, including you, DOING something. Try to draw whole people, not cartoons or stick people. Remember, make everyone DOING something—some kind of action."

SETTING

Provide the child with supplies and instruction and allow the child to draw while you take a history from the parent.

SCORING

Prior to interviewing or performing the pediatric physical exam, pick up the child's drawing and state, "Tell me about your picture." Score the form on the opposite side of the page and determine the course of action (a more focused physical exam and/or child interview alone).

INTERVENTION

If the scored indicators, physical exam and interview lead to suspicion, refer to the appropriate agencies designated by state law.

Projection of the Interpreter into the Drawing

To avoid overinterpretation, it is important that the interpreter's perception of the drawing be unbiased. Look at the picture openly, without judgment initially. Realize that people possess unique psychological frameworks from which to perceive and express their emotional, intellectual and mental content. Do not fall into the trap of impressing your own beliefs onto the interpretation of the work. This is especially easy to do if one has considerable knowledge of the case from parental history. Remain open and allow the child self-expression without interference.

Misinterpretation of Drawing by Child with Impaired Fine Motor Skills

The clinician needs to keep in mind the subject's fine motor ability. Children who have either permanent or temporary impairment in fine motor skills from a disability or injury may not be

FIGURE 7: EXAMPLES OF OVERINTERPRETATION

TABLE 5: QUALITATIVE CONTENT FOR COLOR INTERPRETATION

COLOR	QUALITATIVE MEANING
Red	Vital significance, surging emotions or danger
Pink	Healthy as with skin
Purple	Need for control or support
Orange	Suspenseful, decreasing energy
Blue	Energy
Black	Unknown, fear, threat
Golden Yellow	Something of great value
White	Repressed feelings

Data from Furth, 1988

able to adequately complete the drawing task. Children who have an illness may temporarily draw at a developmentally regressed age. It would be unfair to label a child emotionally disturbed based on inability to draw.

Implications of Color

Qualitative interpretations of color have been made by several investigators including Furth (1988), Luscher (1969), Machover (1949) and Schaie and Heiss (1964). Different theorists do not always agree on the meaning of different colors, but they all suggest that color symbolizes feelings, mood or tone in a picture. When analyzing color, Furth says: "Note where color is used on the page. What is the quantity and the intensity of color displayed?"

Those using a quantitative approach to color indicate that this is a subject not researched, often misinterpreted and based solely on clinical experiences. Just because a child draws with a black crayon does not imply sadness or shame. It may have been the only color available or the child may have another meaning such as darkness during the night (Figure 7). For those interested in the qualitative aspects of color, Table 5 is provided, but we caution you to use discretion. When color is used, a more quantitative approach would be to ask, "What is being emphasized by color?" or "What is being diminished by color?" Further research needs to be done on children's use of color in their HFDs and KFDs (see Afterword).

Chapter 3

The Child Human Figure Drawing Inventory and Interview

Screening Inventory

The Hardin/Peterson form devised for scoring a child's human figure drawing is purely quantitative (see page 40). The scoring is done on the opposite side of the child's drawing. Note that on this form one simply circles whether the indicator is present or absent. The clinician will find that the score form organizes the HFD indicators from most serious to least serious. In addition, the first seven indicators are bolded to highlight what the authors consider to be the "serious seven." The "serious seven" have each been designated 3 points; indicators 8–15 account for 2 points each, and indicators 16–20 are worth 1 point. Indicators 21–28 receive 0.5 points each. Study the HFD inventory form now, as well as the human figure drawing indicators pictured on pages 42–55. These drawings provide instruction as to what is and is not scored using the Hardin/Peterson system of analysis and are designed to assist the reader to see precisely how each indicator is scored. Commit to memory the first seven indicators. Review the child pictures for each HFD indicator, then test yourself using Self-Tests 1–3 on pages 112–117. Once this process is completed, return to the text to read the interview guide, on page 56. This is used when a child's drawing results in a score of either undetermined (3–5 points) or suspicious (6+ points).

When the entire form has been scored (all indicators are circled that are present) from top to bottom, give the drawing a numerical score. Compare that score to the scoring criteria that would result in a referral to a mental health professional.

- Any drawing with a score of over **6** points is **suspicious** and requires an interview, with serious consideration of referral, especially with corroborating findings.
- Any drawing with a score of **3–5** points is **undetermined** and requires an interview with consideration of referral based on additional data retrieved. A follow-up visit and the instruction "Draw me a picture of your family" might assist in this determination.
- A drawing with **0–2** points is considered **normal**.

SCREENING INVENTORY FOR
CHILD HUMAN FIGURE DRAWING

Name: _____ Date: _____ Age: _____

1.	**Explicit drawing of genitalia**	Present (3.0) ....Absent (0)
2.	**Concealment of genitalia**	Present (3.0) ....Absent (0)
3.	**Omission of genital area**	Present (3.0) ....Absent (0)
4.	**Omission of central part of figure**	Present (3.0) ....Absent (0)
5.	**Encapsulation**	Present (3.0) ....Absent (0)
6.	**Fruit trees added**	Present (3.0) ....Absent (0)
7.	**Opposite sex drawn**	Present (3.0) ....Absent (0)
8.	Tiny figure	Present (2.0) ....Absent (0)
9.	Poor integration of body parts/ Monster drawn	Present (2.0) ....Absent (0)
10.	Hands cut off	Present (2.0) ....Absent (0)
11.	Omission of peripheral body parts (arms or legs)	Present (2.0) ....Absent (0)
12.	Belly button added or emphasized	Present (2.0) ....Absent (0)
13.	Jagged teeth	Present (2.0) ....Absent (0)
14.	Big hands	Present (2.0) ....Absent (0)
15.	Transparency	Present (2.0) ....Absent (0)
16.	Slanting figure	Present (1.0) ....Absent (0)
17.	Genitals emphasized	Present (1.0) ....Absent (0)
18.	Legs tightly together	Present (1.0) ....Absent (0)
19.	Waist cut off	Present (1.0) ....Absent (0)
20.	Extensions/Long arms/Long legs	Present (1.0) ....Absent (0)
21.	Rainbows	Present (0.5) ....Absent (0)
22.	Butterflies	Present (0.5) ....Absent (0)
23.	Hearts	Present (0.5) ....Absent (0)
24.	Flying birds	Present (0.5) ....Absent (0)
25.	Rain/Clouds	Present (0.5) ....Absent (0)
26.	Shading of face	Present (0.5) ....Absent (0)
27.	Unicorns	Present (0.5) ....Absent (0)
28.	X for eyes	Present (0.5) ....Absent (0)

Total Overall Score _____

Scoring for this drawing: (check one) ❑ Normal (0-2)   ❑ Undetermined (3-5)   ❑ Suspicious/Refer (6+)

Notes _____
_____
_____

These results are NOT diagnostic for physical, sexual or emotional abuse. The results provide CLUES for the clinician for further investigation by child interview, physical exam and forensic evaluation.   © 1995 Hardin/Peterson

This page may be reproduced without obtaining permission from the publisher or authors.

The interview guide, to be discussed next, will help determine the course of action. The interview should be administered to the child alone in order to elicit more information. If the picture and interview lead to the suspicion of child abuse, follow state reporting regulations. Information elicited from the interview may also help determine what kind of specialized mental health therapy the child may need.

Score the art produced by the child as normal, undetermined or suspicious/refer based on the criteria shown in Table 6. In practice, some cases scored as undetermined warrant a note to obtain another drawing at the next visit. Ask a colleague versed in this scoring method to view and score the same drawing to add to your reliability and validity.

TABLE 6: SCORING HUMAN FIGURE DRAWINGS

Suspicious/Refer . . . . . 6 points
Undetermined . . . . 3-5 points
Normal . . . . 0-2 points

The authors advise that two principles should be followed in using these tools:

- The instructions need to be given verbally to the child by someone who understands the task and can answer any questions the child may have.
- The drawing should be scored while the child is present, in order to ask the child for any information needed to clarify the course of action to be taken, such as the use of the interview.

These principles should be followed by the clinician or clinician assistant, who should ask the child to draw at a small table while the history is taken from the parent. The child should be encouraged to draw with minimal direction. For example, children frequently ask, "Who should I draw?" The response would be, "Whoever you want." Once the child has completed the drawing, his or her picture is used as a bridge to communication. The clinician says, "Let me see your picture." Ideally this is the time to quickly score the form. This will take only a few minutes once the indicators are familiar. One then proceeds to the physical exam or interview. Questions from the interview guide in Table 7 (page 57) can be asked while examining the child's body. If one has any suspicion of sexual or physical abuse, more attention can be given to certain body parts (i.e., genital exam) or more can be asked regarding these parts of the body. Suspicious indicators may also necessitate that the child be interviewed alone. Children will not yield information in the presence of a perpetrator (Elliot & Peterson, 1993). From experience, the authors have found that children cannot come back to a picture a week later, remember and discuss what they drew. Furthermore, waiting a week may evoke recanting if a parent intervenes to silence the child between appointments.

1. EXPLICIT DRAWING OF GENITALIA

Penis, vagina, pubic hair or breasts are frankly displayed or labeled by the child. Even if the clinician does not think the genitalia are depicted as being exposed (naked); and the child says, "This is a penis or breast or vagina," score with the child's interpretation. If one part is concealed and one part explicit, score as explicit display.

Note: Genitals must be located approximately in the proper (correct) places on the body, or labeled by the subject as being genitalia or secondary sex characteristics.

Not scored: Objects in the drawing not in the proper (correct) location of the body which may appear to be penis-, vagina- or breastlike, if not labeled so by the child.

2. CONCEALMENT OF GENITALIA

Drawn objects are placed over specified regions of the body.

Note:
a. Bras, bikinis and shorts are scored here.
b. Objects in the picture or situated in the picture that conceal (hide) either the genital or breast region are scored here.
c. Bras, bikinis and shorts that are shaded **are** scored here.

Not scored:
a. Shading of body parts. If one body part is concealed, but another is explicit, score as explicit.
b. Figures drawn cut off at the waist are not scored here (see 19).
c. Omission of central figure (body) is not scored here (see 4).

3. OMISSION OF GENITAL AREA

Either specified region is omitted in an otherwise complete drawing. Omitted means obviously not drawn in.

Not scored: a. Omission of entire body or figure cut off at the waist is scored elsewhere (see 4 and 19).

             b. Stick figures and tadpole figures are scored elsewhere (see 4 and 9).

4. OMISSION OF CENTRAL PART OF FIGURE

The absence of either the head or body (torso). Tadpole figures are scored here (a head with legs and arms radiating from it).

Not scored: a. Absence of just breast or genital region (see 3).

             b. Stick figures (see 9).

             c. Absence of limbs (see 11). Normal for children 3–5 years of age.

             d. Figures cut off at waist (see p. 19).

5. ENCAPSULATION

The figure is either partially or completely enclosed by a drawn line or lines.

Note: a. Any attempt to enclose, "wall off" or compartmentalize the principal figure in the drawing is scored as an encapsulation.

   b. A figure that is totally or almost totally enclosed by shading, as if darkness, is scored as an encapsulation.

   c. Items used to enclose a figure, such as houses, swing sets, etc., are considered to be encapsulations.

6. FRUIT TREES ADDED

A fruit tree is spontaneously added to the drawing by the child.

Note: The tree should obviously be a fruit tree (any variety) or designated as a fruit tree by the artist.

Not scored: a. Pine trees
   b. Coconut trees
   c. Palm trees

7. OPPOSITE SEX DRAWN

The figure is the opposite sex from the child.

Note: The drawn figure is obviously the opposite sex of the child or identified by the child as being the opposite sex.

Example: (BY FEMALE) Obvious male figure or identified as male by artist.

8. TINY FIGURE

Figure is 3 inches or less in height.

9. POOR INTEGRATION OF BODY PARTS/MONSTER DRAWN

The human figure is distorted in appearance. There is some slight tolerance allowed for "imperfect" drawing, but **out-of-proportion** body parts, in relation to the whole figure, are considered distortions.

Note:
a. Stick figures, including **clothed** stick figures are scored here.
b. Monster-looking figures are scored here.
c. Scattered body parts are scored here.

Not scored:
a. Tadpole figures (see 4).
b. Big hands in drawing (see 14).
c. Tiny figure (see 8).
d. Out-of-proportion genitals (see 17).
e. Figures missing body parts (see 10, 11 and 19).
f. Out-of-proportion hand.

10. HANDS CUT OFF

The arms are drawn in the picture, but the hand (or hands) are not.

Note:
a. **Either** hand can be missing and counted as hands cut off.
b. Hands drawn in pockets or behind the back **are** counted as hand cut off.

Not scored:
a. Mitten-type hands at the end of 2-dimensional arms, which are indicated by a line, are **not** scored here (see 14).
b. The absence of the entire body, **including hands**, is not scored here (see 4).
c. The absence of arms, **including hands,** is not scored here (see 11).
d. Lines drawn to portray fingers at the end of a single or double line arm are **not** scored here.

11. OMISSION OF PERIPHERAL BODY PARTS (ARMS OR LEGS)

Either arms or legs are not drawn.

Note: The absence of only one arm or leg **is** enough to score this as an omission of peripheral body parts. Body parts (arms and legs) that are drawn but not attached to the central body part are still counted as peripheral body parts.

Not scored:
a. If whole body is missing, this is **not** scored here (see 4).
b. Absence of hands is **not** scored here (see 10).
c. Absence of feet is **not** scored here.
d. Winglike arms are **not** scored here (see 14).
e. Detached (but drawn) arms and legs are **not** scored here (see 9).

12. BELLY BUTTON ADDED OR EMPHASIZED

Belly button (navel) is visibly present in the drawing or labeled as being present by the child.

Note: Belly button **must** be in lower abdomen area, unless labeled as being elsewhere.

Not scored: Buttons on the human figure drawing which are part of clothing.

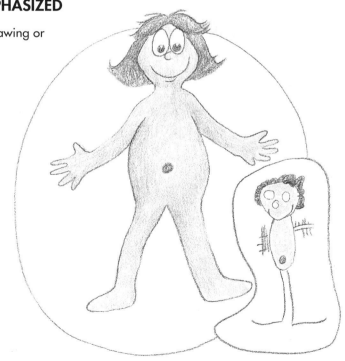

13. JAGGED TEETH

Full mouth drawn with teeth emphasis. Mouth drawn down with sawtooth configuration.

14. BIG HANDS

Hands are **almost** as big or bigger than the face of the figure.

Note:
  a. Large arms that are **winglike** in appearance are scored here.
  b. If figure has only one big hand, it is still scored as big hands.
  c. Winglike arms are considered arms and hands **and** should be scored as big hands.

15. TRANSPARENCY

Either:

1. The outline of a figure with clothes drawn around the figure or
2. Ordinary drawing with focus on one particular portion of the figure visible through the drawn clothing.

Note: If body is visible under **shaded** clothing, code as transparency.

16. SLANTING FIGURE

The axis of the figure is tilted by 15° or more. The figure seems to be on the verge of falling over, whether doing an activity or not. Figures that are leaning on some object **should** be scored as slanting if at 15° or more angle.

Not scored: Figure lying down **completely** horizontal.

17. GENITALS EMPHASIZED

Emphasis of penis, vagina, breasts or buttocks through heavy line stroke, overdetailing or enlargement.

Note: a. Zippers on trousers are scored here.
            b. Hour-glass shape exaggeration is scored here.
            c. Drawn genitalia which are **not** obviously naked are scored here.

Not scored: **Naked,** explicit genitalia or secondary sex characteristics (see 1).

18. LEGS TIGHTLY TOGETHER

A single line is drawn to indicate two 2-dimensional legs pressed together.

19. WAIST CUT OFF

Lower portion of body is absent due to either the bottom edge of the paper or the lower portion of the body not being drawn.

Note: The figure does **not** have to cut off **exactly** at the waist. It can be cut off a little lower or a little higher.

Not scored:
a. **Only** legs cut off is scored elsewhere (see 11).
b. Absence of limbs is **not** scored here (see 11).
c. Absence of body (whole) is **not** scored here (see 4).

20. EXTENSIONS/LONG ARMS/LONG LEGS

Long arms or legs or lines or rackets or sports equipment. Not only something held in the hand but also something rigid and solid that can be controlled by the child to keep a distance (bats, vaccum, broom). An article such as a balloon or kite that is out of the child's control does not constitute an extension.

21. RAINBOWS

A rainbow is spontaneously added to the drawing by the artist.

Note: There needs to be **more** than one line to indicate the representation of a rainbow, unless specified as such by the artist.

22. BUTTERFLIES

A butterfly is spontaneously added to the drawing by the child.

Note:
a. The butterfly should obviously be a butterfly or designated as such by the child.
b. A butterfly that is a decal, insignia, or design on the human figure's clothing is scored here.
c. The presence of even **one** butterfly is enough to score this.

Not scored: Single lines representing flying animals are **not** scored here (see 24).

23. HEARTS

A heart is spontaneously added to the drawing by the child.

Note: a. The heart **can** be represented anywhere on the drawing.
b. Valentine hearts are represented here.

Not scored: Anatomical hearts drawn to indicate the biological organs of the human figures depicted are **not** scored here.

24. FLYING BIRDS

A flying bird is spontaneously added to the drawing by the child.

Note: Any representation of a flying bird (or birds) is scored here.

Not scored: A bird that is not flying is **not** scored.

25. RAIN/CLOUDS

Rain or clouds are added spontaneously to the drawing.

26. SHADING OF FACE

Not scored: Erasures or smudging of face.
Shading that depicts skin color.

27. UNICORNS

Any depiction or labeling of a drawing as containing a unicorn, that is, a horse with a horn protruding from its forehead.

28. X FOR EYES

Score only if both eyes have an X drawn in an oval or round eye.

Interview Guide

Children find the interview an unnatural means of communicating. They are action oriented and often feel uncomfortable verbalizing their problems. They may not have the vocabulary or experience to put their thoughts into words, even though the concepts are fairly well-formed. Trusting an unfamiliar adult is not easy. Often children are confused about why a clinician wants to talk with them, even about a picture. They may believe they have been bad or are being singled out in some way. Discussing self or family problems may be feared as disloyal behavior that could result in punishment or guilt. Therefore, they require "wooing" to reveal their perceptions. The clinician's patience will be rewarded, however, because children have fewer "masks" than adults and will often give the clinician information denied or deleted by adult caretakers.

The authors have found the following approach achieves the best results, and have organized the human figure and kinetic family drawing interview guides accordingly:

- Use simple, concrete language.
- Assume an attitude of fun, exploration and enthusiasm.
- Balance providing a sense of direction with following the lead of the child.
- Give reassurance, act interested, take the child's point of reference.
- Don't pass judgment, good or bad, on what the child says.
- Use third person or impersonal questions, rather than direct questions.
- Establish the universality of feelings such as: "Some kids are afraid of things they don't understand" or "Sometimes kids find . . . "
- Use the child's language and frame of reference to follow up on subjects the child initiates.
- Conduct more than one interview.
- Maintain confidentiality and child advocacy until certain of information.
- Rehearse with the child how and what will be revealed to adult caretakers.
- Anticipate adult action or backlash against the child and clinician for revealed information.

The human figure drawing interview guide, in Table 7, is organized in sequence from the easiest to the most difficult questions one would ask a child. The clinical interview commences with the child's art production and proceeds to an examination of the child. The clinician needs to be careful to refer to the picture, not the artist. For example, in question 4 the clinician asks, "What is this person doing?" rather than "What are you doing?" This technique allows the child to emotionally distance from the picture, even if it is a self-portrait. Additionally, the interview form provides explicit instructions to deal with a child's responses to the interview. For example, in question 9, the clinician asks, "What does this person in the picture need most?" If the child gives a material example such as "roller skates" or "Nintendo," it is usually a typical answer. If the child says, "a daddy" or "more love," there are probably emotional needs. Note that in this above question the word "person" is used rather than a name or sex (i.e., "What does this girl need most?"). This allows the child to respond indirectly, which usually reveals more information. To talk about a person (questions 3, 4, 9, 10) or a picture (questions 1, 5) does not require revealing information that the child might feel is confidential or potentially damaging. Ten questions are asked

TABLE 7: INTERVIEW GUIDE TO HUMAN FIGURE DRAWINGS

INSTRUCTIONS: Before beginning this interview, determine if the child is in therapy and if so, where in the course of therapy as this interview may not be applicable. Indicators may be present because the child is "working through" problems.

1. "Let's talk about your picture." (Place drawing in front of the child. Remove pencils, pens or markers so child cannot amend as you discuss.)

2. "Is this a boy or a girl?"

3. "How old is this person?" (Use person, not a name or sex. Avoid "How old is this girl?")

4. "What is this person doing?" If a child says, "I don't know," follow with, "Well, it's your drawing. What would they be doing?" (Allow the child to create a story. Remember children may be fearful of relating family secrets or speaking negatively for fear of being "found out" and punished. The question about this picture should be approached like a game.) Accept what the child says.

5. "In this picture is this person happy or sad?" (Talk about the picture; otherwise the child might think about the real person at another time.) If child says, "Happy," ask #6.

6. "Is this person happy or sad on the inside too?"

7. "What's the best body part?"

8. "What's the worst body part?" If child says, "Nothing," reply with, "Everyone has parts they like better or worse than others."

9. "What does this person in the picture need most?" If the child gives a material answer such as "roller skates" or "Nintendo," it is usually a normal child answer. If the child says, "A Daddy" or "More love," there are probably emotional needs.

10. "Does this person in the picture ever feel so sad he or she feels like dying?"

11. "Have you ever been too sad to eat?" " . . . too sad to sleep?" " . . . too sad to play?"

12. "Do you have nightmares?" If "yes," ask, "Do you tell anyone about your nightmares?"

13. "What's the worst thing that could happen to someone?"

14. "What's the worst thing a person could do?"

15. "What's the worst thing you ever did?"

16. "What's the worst thing that has happened to you?" If child says, "Nothing," say to the child, "Everyone has something bad that happens."

17. "Have you ever thought about hurting yourself?" If "yes," ask, "What did you do?"

18. "Have you ever wished you were never born?"

19. "What's the best thing that ever happened to you?"

NOTE: Refer to a trained professional if the questions above lead you to a concern about the child experiencing either sexual or physical abuse. If child answers #14 by saying, "Dad asked me to touch his pee pee," refer according to state law requirements. If you are not specifically trained, don't ask for more detail because this may contaminate a pending investigation.

If you have time for only three questions, ask:

1. "If you had three wishes, what would they be?"

2. "Do you think things are getting better or worse?"

3. "If it were up to you, what would you like me to do? Do you ever wish people would just stop asking you questions about this?"

before any personal information is elicited. The clinician can select those questions that seem relevant from questions 11–19. The authors recommend that one always end with a positive question, such as number 19: "What's the best thing that ever happened to you?" Additionally, three questions are listed at the end of the interview, which can be quite revealing and especially useful in a busy classroom, family medicine or pediatric practice when a full interview is difficult to conduct. These questions are helpful to ask with the child alone: 1, "If you had three wishes, what would they be?" 2, "Do you think things are getting better or worse?" and finally, 3, "If it were up to you, what would you like me to do? Do you ever wish people would just stop asking you questions about this?"

Chapter 4

The Child Kinetic Family Drawing Inventory and Interview

Screening Inventory

The interaction or lack of interaction among family members in a child's drawing sugests the interpersonal communication and type of activities families engage in together. The KFD shows the child's perception of emotional support displayed between family members. This form of drawing differs from the HFD in that it includes both qualitative and quantitative indicators. The scoring method incorporates the added complexity of the KFD drawings. For example, the clinician must evaluate the interaction between family members as well as the child's perception of relationships and power structures within the family. On the Peterson/Hardin KFD form, the first three sectors are purely qualitative: quality of the overall drawing, child's perception of family members, and child's perception of self. The approach to these sectors is similar to the mental status exam or the initial physical appraisal of the body. One evaluates the global picture or person before proceeding to the fine detail of symmetry, deviation from norm or unusual features (see Table 8).

TABLE 8: BASIC CONCEPTS OF QUALITATIVE KFD INTERPRETATION

1. Concentrate on the initial feeling you get looking at the drawing. Is the mood happy, sad, angry? Is the work orderly or chaotic? Does anything appear strange or peculiar?

2. Act as a researcher; look at size, shape and distortion of figures drawn. Note the direction of movement of characters.

3. Address focal points—missing items, added features and areas of emphasis.

4. Tabulate individual indicators into a hypothesis considering the child's history and interview responses.

Data from Furth, 1988

The screening inventory for kinetic family drawing is introduced on page 61. In the qualitative sectors, the authors have used the designation of red, yellow and green to assist the clinician to discriminate deviation from normal. These discriminators follow the analogy of the street light. When a red indicator appears, one should stop, look and listen to what the child is attempting to communicate nonverbally. When yellow indicators are present, one should approach the task with caution, slow down and provide time for the child to amplify his expression verbally by saying: "Tell me more about your picture." The "green light" indicators refer to a normal or expected outcome indicating that it is safe to go on or proceed to the task at hand. Note that the *quality of overall drawing* refers to any peculiarity, mood or disorder in the drawing. The three pictures on pages 66, 68 and 70 show the reader each of these factors on a separate page. Note on page 70, for example, the difference between order and disorder, graduated by intensity in the drawings.

Similarly, mood is shown on page 68 and peculiarity on page 76. The evaluator must make a subjective interpretation of these factors as they apply to the child's drawing of his or her family doing something. Next, the evaluator proceeds to the last three sectors of the drawing, which are, like the HFD, completely quantitative, circling those indicators present or absent and tabulating a score.

In summary, one approaches the KFD from the top of the form to make an overall qualitative appraisal of the art work. To actually score and interpret the work, however, the evaluator tabulates the number of quantitative indicators in the *styles* sector first, then the *treatment of figures,* and finally, *actions with negative aspects.* Table 9 outlines scoring kinetic family drawings. Note that in all sectors indicators are listed from most to least serious. In the *styles* sector, encapsulation and compartmentalization are accorded 2 points each; writing words on the picture and edging receive 1 point each; and underlining or lining at top or bottom of the paper are each given ½ point. Similarly, under *treatment of figures,* the first two indicators, transparency and missing person or self, receive 2 points each; indicators 3–6 (one or more figures drawn on back of paper, erasures, floating and hanging) are accorded 1 point; and indicators 7–10 (falling, slanting figure, incomplete figures and extensions) deserve ½ point each. Finally, under *actions with negative aspects,* indicators 1–3 (sexualized, aggression/weapons, and fear/anxiety) receive 2 points each; indicators 4 and 5 (withdrawal/isolation, blaming/ridicule) receive 1 point each; and indicators 6 and 7 (submission/competition, barriers) receive ½ point each. The clinician tabulates the child's results and gives an overall score of normal (0–2 points), undetermined (3–5 points), or suspicious/refer (6+). When the quantitative section is tabulated, one would conduct a KFD interview for any score over 3 points (both for undetermined and suspicious scores).

The qualitative section of the KFD shows
the global picture before proceeding to the fine
discrimination of the quantitative section.

SCREENING INVENTORY FOR KINETIC FAMILY DRAWING

Name: _____   Date: _____   Age: _____

	RED FLAGS	YELLOW FLAGS	GREEN FLAGS

Qualitative

I.   QUALITY OF OVERALL DRAWING

		RED FLAGS	YELLOW FLAGS	GREEN FLAGS
1)	Peculiarity/Strangeness	☐ Very peculiar	☐ Somewhat peculiar	☐ Not at all peculiar
2)	Feeling/Mood	☐ Depressed/Angry	☐ Mixed emotions	☐ Happy/Content
3)	Order	☐ Unorganized	☐ Partially organized	☐ Orderly

II. CHILD PERCEPTION OF FAMILY MEMBERS

		RED FLAGS	YELLOW FLAGS	GREEN FLAGS
1)	Size	☐ Very disproportionate	☐ Some disproportion	☐ Proportionate
2)	Shape	☐ Very disproportionate	☐ Some disproportion	☐ Proportionate
3)	Distortion	☐ Excessive	☐ Some	☐ None

III. CHILD SELF-PERCEPTION IN FAMILY SYSTEM

		RED FLAGS	YELLOW FLAGS	GREEN FLAGS
1)	Size	☐ Very disproportionate	☐ Some disproportion	☐ Proportionate
2)	Shape	☐ Very disproportionate	☐ Some disproportion	☐ Proportionate
3)	Distortion	☐ Excessive	☐ Some	☐ None

Because of the complexity of the KFD and the lack of quantification for peculiarity and order, always interview the child if the drawing shows excessive disorder (chaos) or peculiarity, as these are not factored in the scoring system.

Quantitative

IV. STYLES (Note which figure on dotted line)

1)	Encapsulation	Present (2.0)	Absent (0)
2)	Compartmentalization	Present (2.0)	Absent (0)
3)	Writing words on picture	Present (1.0)	Absent (0)
4)	Edging	Present (1.0)	Absent (0)
5)	Underlining individual figures	Present (0.5)	Absent (0)
6)	Lining at top of paper	Present (0.5)	Absent (0)
7)	Lining at bottom of paper	Present (0.5)	Absent (0)

V.   TREATMENT OF FIGURES (Note which figure on dotted line)

1)	Transparency	Present (2.0)	Absent (0)
2)	Missing person or self	Present (2.0)	Absent (0)
3)	One or more figures drawn on back of paper	Present (1.0)	Absent (0)
4)	Erasures	Present (1.0)	Absent (0)
5)	Floating	Present (1.0)	Absent (0)
6)	Hanging	Present (1.0)	Absent (0)
7)	Falling	Present (0.5)	Absent (0)
8)	Slanting figures	Present (0.5)	Absent (0)
9)	Incomplete figures (omission of parts)	Present (0.5)	Absent (0)
10)	Extensions/Long legs, arms, equipment	Present (0.5)	Absent (0)

VI. ACTIONS WITH NEGATIVE ASPECTS (Note which figure on dotted line)

1)	Sexualized	Present (2.0)	Absent (0)
2)	Aggression/Weapons	Present (2.0)	Absent (0)
3)	Fear/Anxiety	Present (2.0)	Absent (0)
4)	Withdrawal/Isolation	Present (1.0)	Absent (0)
5)	Blame/Ridicule	Present (1.0)	Absent (0)
6)	Submission/Competition	Present (0.5)	Absent (0)
7)	Barriers	Present (0.5)	Absent (0)

☐ **Normal (0-2)**   ☐ **Undetermined (3-5)**   ☐ **Suspicious/Refer (6+)**   **TOTAL OVERALL SCORE:** _____

Notes _____

These results are NOT diagnostic for physical, sexual or emotional abuse. The results provide CLUES for the clinician for further investigation by child interview, physical exam and forensic evaluation.

© 1995 Peterson/Hardin
(Adapted from Burns & Kaufman, 1972)

This page may be reproduced without obtaining permission from the publisher or authors.

TABLE 9
SCORING KINETIC FAMILY DRAWINGS

START at the top of the inventory. Score all six of the sectors by circling items in each sector that are present or absent.

I.   **Quality of overall drawing**
     Note whether the drawing appears peculiar (unusual) in any way. Is there any disorganization or was the picture completed in an orderly fashion? What is the overall mood of the picture: depressed/angry; mixed emotions; happy/content?

II. **Child perception of family members**
     Observe size, shape and distortion for each family member. Are they drawn realistically?

III. **Child self-perception in family system**
     Next look at how the child portrays himself/herself in relationship to the family members. Observe his/her size, shape or distortion in relationship to each family member. Does he/she portray reality?

IV. **Styles**
     1 & 2 are serious indicators, given a score of 2 points each. 3 & 4 are moderate indicators, given a score of 1 point each. 5-7 are scored ½ point each.

V.   **Treatment of figures**
     1 & 2 are serious indicators, given a score of 2 points each. 3-6 are moderate indicators, given a score of 1 point each. 7-10 are scored ½ point each.

VI. **Actions with negative aspects**
     1-3 are serious indicators, given a score of 2 points each. 3-5 are moderate indicators, given a score of 1 point each. 5-7 are scored ½ point each.

Scoring for this drawing: (check one)

❏ **Normal (0-2)**   ❏ **Undetermined (3-5)**   ❏ **Suspicious/Refer (6+)**

NOTE: If the drawing has no indicators in sectors IV, V and VI—but does have problems in sectors I, II or III, rule out perceptual or motor disabilities, such as developmental vision problems, or dysfunctions, such as muscular dystrophy, cerebral palsy, etc. These first three sectors may also give clues to children with lower mental functioning for chronological age or children experiencing emotional or situational stress, such as divorce.

FIGURE 8. CHRISTY'S DRAWING

In order to use the KFD inventory, consider the following application. When assessing the *child self-perception,* note his or her relationship to other family members, including size, shape or distortion. Do these factors portray reality? Is he or she really that small or tall? Note how Christy, age 7, designates herself with her other siblings in Figure 8. Although she is only a year younger than her older sister, she draws herself small, distorted and shaded over. When assessing the *child perception of family members,* note size, shape and distortion. Also determine the order in which members were drawn and the direction of movement, noting any closeness or isolation depicted. Using Christy's drawing, note that Mary and Dena are drawn larger than Christy herself, in spite of the fact that Mary is only 4 years old and Dena is 8. Note that Dad is drawn small, although in reality he is 6'4" and Mom is only 5'2". Note the lines that separate the family from each other, designating a lack of closeness. Finally, note the *quality of overall drawing.* Is it disorganized or orderly? What is the overall mood one has when viewing it (i.e., depressed/angry, mixed emotions or happy/content)? Is there anything peculiar? Using the KFD inventory, attempt to score Christy's picture now. The next page shows the way the authors would score her production.

SCREENING INVENTORY FOR KINETIC FAMILY DRAWING
Scoring of Christy's Drawing by the Authors

Name: __Christy__   Date: __2/31/1990__   Age: ____7____

	RED FLAGS	**YELLOW FLAGS**	**GREEN FLAGS**

Qualitative

I.   QUALITY OF OVERALL DRAWING
1) Peculiarity/Strangeness — ☐ Very peculiar — ☑ Somewhat peculiar — ☐ Not at all peculiar
2) Feeling/Mood — ☐ Depressed/Angry — ☑ Mixed emotions — ☐ Happy/Content
3) Order — ☐ Unorganized — ☐ Partially organized — ☑ Orderly

II.   CHILD PERCEPTION OF FAMILY MEMBERS
1) Size — ☑ Very disproportionate — ☐ Some disproportion — ☐ Proportionate
2) Shape — ☐ Very disproportionate — ☐ Some disproportion — ☑ Proportionate
3) Distortion — ☐ Excessive — ☑ Some — ☐ None

III.   CHILD SELF-PERCEPTION IN FAMILY SYSTEM
1) Size — ☐ Very disproportionate — ☑ Some disproportion — ☐ Proportionate
2) Shape — ☐ Very disproportionate — ☐ Some disproportion — ☑ Proportionate
3) Distortion — ☐ Excessive — ☐ Some — ☑ None

Because of the complexity of the KFD and the lack of quantification for peculiarity and order, always interview the child if the drawing shows excessive disorder (chaos) or peculiarity, as these are not factored in the scoring system.

Quantitative

IV.   STYLES (Note which figure on dotted line)
1) Encapsulation — Present (2.0) ....Absent (0)
2) Compartmentalization — (Present (2.0)) ...."mommy" and "daddy"..................Absent (0)
3) Writing words on picture — Present (1.0) ....Absent (0)
4) Edging — Present (1.0) ....Absent (0)
5) Underlining individual figures — Present (0.5) ....Absent (0)
6) Lining at top of paper — Present (0.5) ....Absent (0)
7) Lining at bottom of paper — Present (0.5) ....Absent (0)

V.   TREATMENT OF FIGURES (Note which figure on dotted line)
1) Transparency — Present (2.0) ....Absent (0)
2) Missing person or self — Present (2.0) ....Absent (0)
3) One or more figures drawn on back of paper — Present (1.0) ....Absent (0)
4) Erasures — Present (1.0) ....Absent (0)
5) Floating — (Present (1.0)) ..all but "mommy"..................................Absent (0)
6) Hanging — Present (1.0) ....Absent (0)
7) Falling — Present (0.5) ....Absent (0)
8) Slanting figures — Present (0.5) ....Absent (0)
9) Incomplete figures (omission of parts) — Present (0.5) ....Absent (0)
10) Extensions/Long legs, arms, equipment — (Present (0.5)) ..all but "mommy" and "Dena"..........Absent (0)

VI.   ACTIONS WITH NEGATIVE ASPECTS (Note which figure on dotted line)
1) Sexualized — Present (2.0) ....Absent (0)
2) Aggression/Weapons — Present (2.0) ....Absent (0)
3) Fear/Anxiety — Present (2.0) ....Absent (0)
4) Withdrawal/Isolation — Present (1.0) ....Absent (0)
5) Blame/Ridicule — Present (1.0) ....Absent (0)
6) Submission/Competition — Present (0.5) ....Absent (0)
7) Barriers — Present (0.5) ....Absent (0)

☐ Normal (0-2)   ☑ Undetermined (3-5)   ☐ Suspicious/Refer (6+)   **TOTAL OVERALL SCORE:** ___3.5___

Notes _____

At this point, review all of the KFD illustrations on the following pages representing each of the six KFD sectors. A brief case description is given for each KFD. These case descriptions have been altered to protect the identity of each family. Note that if a child has no indicators in sectors 4, 5 or 6, but does show problems in sectors 1, 2 or 3, perceptual or motor disabilities, such as developmental vision problems, or other dysfunctions, such as muscular dystrophy, mild head injury, attention deficit or cerebral palsy, might be present. A less orderly or lower quality picture may also reflect lack of skill in artistic production or lower mental functioning for chronological age. Finally, unusual productions in the three qualitative sectors may be due to children's experiencing situational emotional stress such as occurs in divorce or custody battles. In such cases, the clinician should consider additional qualitative features, including:

- *Size* (power versus lack of power; value versus devalue). Figures drawn proportionately larger or smaller than their relative size in the family may reflect the artist's regard for those family members.
- *Order drawn* (value versus devalue). The order in which the child draws the family indicates how he or she recalls, and decides to include, each family member and may reflect the importance of each family member. Drawing the self first is not unusual in young children.
- *Position* (connection versus distance). The proximity or distance of figures may reflect the child's perception of emotional closeness (or distance) between family members.
- *Similarity of same-gender family members* (sexual identification). The child's different depictions of family members of the same sex may reflect his or her perception of sexual identification throughout the family.
- *Direction of movement* (ways of relating to each other). Figures drawn showing movement toward and away from each other may reflect the child's perception of relationships between family members. The relationship may be positive or negative in nature. Movement between figures may be depicted by objects, such as balls or ropes, or by activities identified by the child, such as "cooking together" or "playing."

I. QUALITY OF OVERALL DRAWING: Peculiarity/Strangeness

A KFD drawing may be peculiar even though a visual inspection (examination) of the drawing does not necessarily reveal oddities. A blind rater may judge a particular KFD as being **not at all peculiar**. It is context that is important. If the child produces a KFD of all the dead members of his or her family, this would make the drawing **very peculiar**. It is important to score peculiarity/strangeness according to what the clinician knows about the family.

Very Peculiar

A 5-year-old girl produces a drawing after the sudden death of her younger brother to whom she was very close. The brother died of leukemia and was at home for his final hours of life. The family had not explained to her the concept of death or her brother's expected fate. He died while she was at school, and his body was removed before she returned home. Erroneously the parents thought they were "protecting her." As a result, the young girl refused to attend school, fearful of further losses. Note the peculiarity of the brother's body depicted with broken lines, standing on the baseline, holding her hand which has not yet let go of him.

Somewhat peculiar

The viewer sees what appears to be a "happy picture" with a smiling child, a little bird and the sun shining. The unicorn has stars around his crown. On closer inspection one notes a peculiar long arm which is keeping the animal at a distance. This 11-year-old girl later revealed in interview that she had experienced incest during a visit to her estranged father.

Not at all peculiar

I. QUALITY OF OVERALL DRAWING: Feeling/Mood

A KFD may be scored on this quality not only from facial expressions, depicted actions and descriptive words on the paper, but also from spontaneous environmental additions to the KFD by the child. The clinician should pay attention to the presence of dark clouds over family members, thorn bushes and other similar additions. Marks on the KFD are often ambiguous or unknown to the examiner. The clinician should ask the child about any questionable marks.

Depressed/Angry

This 10-year-old girl depicts her anger and depression regarding the recent divorce of her parents. Note that the parents are turned away from the child. The child writes words on the picture to emphasize her feelings, while her parents engage in dialogue with each other. Note the child's down-turned mouth and tears denoting sadness. The word "No" depicts anger. A divorce paper with a dark zigzag appearance adds another dimension of depression and anger.

Mixed emotions

This 9-year-old girl shows mixed emotions. All family members except Dad are shown with happy faces. Dad and daughter are highlighted by the placement of a rainbow over their heads. The artist cannot reach her father with the tiny barrier between them. This drawing was made after the child's father died of liver cancer (the area of emphasis is on the father figure).

Happy/Content

I. QUALITY OF OVERALL DRAWING: Order

This quality is scored by assessing the entire drawing. Order in the drawing is determined by the placement of people, objects, words and other marks on the paper. Excessive detail or even clutter may not be unorganized, depending on the child's approach to the task. The KFD must have little or no organization to be scored unorganized.

Unorganized

This 8-year-old boy sustained an accident in which he and his 10-year-old sister were pro-pelled into a field from a camper/trailer when their aunt, who was driving, collided with a cow crossing the highway. The children had been playing in the rear camper when the impact took place. The camper became detached from the truck and made several circular excursions before landing. The boy's sister died from the accident and the artist sustained a broken leg and tissue injury. His picture depicts the chaos experienced in frequent nightmares associated with his posttraumatic response to this event. The unorganized aspects of the picture include the shoes, bottles and debris shown in mid-air. Bodies are scattered on the ground. The truck is overturned. Drawing this picture assisted him to be free of nightmares within several weeks.

Partially organized

This 9-year-old girl goes on visitation to her father and is molested in his bedroom. The drawing tells a story in a sequence. The sequence moves both horizontally and vertically. The words and lines on the page add confusion to the organization.

Orderly

The brother (age 7 years) of the 9-year-old girl who drew the above "partially organized" drawing created a convergent organized family picture. He was the father's favorite child and experienced no molesta-tion.

II. CHILD PERCEPTION OF FAMILY MEMBERS

The dimensions of **size, shape and distortion** are scored according to how the child depicts or omits family members. Inclusion of extended family members, pets and friends may indicate significance of that person/animal to the child. The dimensions of size and shape relate to the child's accurate reproduction of family members. Distortion relates to perceptual differences other than size and shape that make the family member(s) appear unusual or inaccurate.

A

B

Child Perception of Family Members

A The artist, Christy, is 7 years old; her sister Dena is 8 and Mary is 4. There is a discrepancy in size among the children and adults. In reality Christy is about the same size as Dena, and Mary is considerably smaller. A very disproportionate size exists between Mother and Father: Christy's Mother is actually 5'2" and Dad is 6'4".

Note the shape of the arms on Mary and Dad, which exceed the length of those of other family members. Note the distortion in Mary's arms. The length of the father's arms set him apart from other family members. The white area below Mom's neck is a distortion. Although the arms on the mother are proportionate to her body size, they are significantly smaller than Dad's and Mary's arms. Shapes are essentially the same. Note in particular that the shape of Dad and Christy are the same.

This child was initially referred for learning difficulties by her school counselor. Upon testing, it was discovered that she was very bright for her age, but highly influenced by the dynamics in the family. Mom was enduring domestic violence from Dad. Dad had just lost his long-term executive position and was unhappy to be employed as a truck driver. His sadness and aggressive arms are clearly shown. Christy shows her angry mouth and later reveals that Dad is physically abusing her, but not the other girls. Mary is perceived as "getting all the attention," and Dena is admired for "being a good student" in school.

B Dena, age 8, draws the same family through her perception as the oldest daughter. This is an orderly, accurate and proportionate drawing showing no indicators.

III.   CHILD SELF-PERCEPTION IN FAMILY SYSTEM

The **size, shape and distortion** dimensions are scored for accuracy as with the child perception of family members. The clinician should score these dimensions based on how the artist depicts the self in relation to the other family members.

A

B

Child Self-Perception in Family System

A This 10-year-old girl draws all members in proportion and with shapes and sizes that approximate reality. Dad, who is a physician, is actually a man of short stature; the mother is somewhat taller. The artist is the oldest daughter, with a sister, age 8, and the brother, age 5, next to herself. The fourth child is an infant who is placed apart from the family.

The artist designates herself by writing "Me" under her picture. She is referred because her mother thinks she is already too much of a perfectionist. In this family the artist, who has a bow on her head, is the only one who performs as a ballerina. Note that she has no arms, however, to reach out and she places herself in the midst of her siblings. In actuality, she assumes much of the child care, as the youngest child is an infant with cystic fibrosis demanding much of her mother's time. Note that both parents have arms, but they are drawn held to the sides of their bodies. All of the children are without arms. By interview it is discovered that since the birth of the baby everyone is restricted from activities that were formerly enjoyed by the family.

B In this drawing the 5-year-old child correctly draws the proportion and size of her parents, but denotes herself smaller than her infant brother whom she perceives to have much of the power. She has no arms, whereas all other family members have arms. She correctly perceives her sexual identity with her mother. The fact that the child gives all family members but herself a face, which she shades, deserves further investigation through interview.

IV. STYLES: Encapsulation

This is scored when drawn lines, objects or walls completely enclose one or more individuals, separating them from the rest of the family. The lines must be incorporated within the drawing to be scored as encapsulation. Both encapsulation and compartmentalization can occur in the same KFD.

IV. STYLES: Compartmentalization

This is scored when one or more family members are isolated from each other with lines, objects or walls that extend to (or close to) the edges of the paper. Both encapsulation and compartmentalization can occur in the same KFD.

Encapsulation

A 7-year-old boy draws an encapsulation around himself at the window and around each of his two friends. This picture is completed after the abduction and kidnapping of two classmates who lived across the street from the artist. The two classmates were kidnapped from the bus stop near the artist's home.

Compartmentalization

The artist, a 6-year-old boy, draws both pictures of himself alone and his parents with his older brother on the same piece of paper. Mom and Dad are both physicians with busy schedules who have recently spent every evening with their older son (Jeff) helping him with homework, due to his learning difficulties.

Prior to the drawing of this picture, the parents were unaware that the younger boy (who had no learning problems) felt temporarily "cut off" from the family. One week later, when the parents equalized their attention to both boys, the artist drew the family all together and removed the compartments.

IV. STYLES: Writing words on picture

This is scored when the child writes on the drawing, using dialogue, comments and labels (including emotions). This does not include family names or labels such as "cat," "dog," etc. to depict family pets. Other labels should be scored here.

IV. STYLES: Edging

This is scored when the family members are placed by the child on the periphery of the paper in an edging or rectangular style. The placement of the figures must be on at least two different edges of the paper. Figures aligned only along the baseline of the paper are not scored as edging.

Writing words on picture

A 10-year-old boy, when asked to draw a picture of his family, simply wrote on the page his explicit feeling about his diagnosis. In interview, he revealed how the disease had affected everyone and he felt responsible.

Edging

The 7-year-old artist, the girl facing the reader, hesitates in discussing the man depicted on the edge of the reader's left side. The child is one of four siblings, two of whom are twin girls at the top of the page, and one of whom is a younger brother on the right side of the page. She reveals only that the person she has the most trouble with is her "Dad," to whom she points on the left margin. The mother is notably missing from the picture due to a prolonged absence and hospitalization. The father is attempting to keep the family "going" but has had little experience with the day-to-day running of the household. The child "hedges" about the adult expectations placed upon her, the oldest daughter, since the mother's absence.

IV. STYLES: Underlining individual figures

This is scored when one or more figures are underscored by a line or shaded area. A solid line or edge of the paper used as a common baseline for the figures is not scored here.

Underlining individual figures

A 6-year-old girl underlines her mother and herself as the most significant, grounded figures. Note that the father is not underlined. The child relates in interview that her father seldom makes decisions.

IV. STYLES: Lining at top of paper

This is scored when the child draws lines or shading across the top of the paper or the heads of the drawn figures. Dark lines described as "clouds" should be scored here if the lines extend across the top of the paper or over the heads of the drawn figures.

IV. STYLES: Lining on bottom of paper

This is scored when the child draws a line or lines across the bottom of the paper or under the feet of all the drawn figures. Individual lines drawn under figures are not scored here. Figures drawn along the baseline of the paper without a drawn line are not scored here.

Lining at top of paper

A child, age 5 years, draws himself with his father who has just lost his corporate job. The son says to the clinician, "I'm saying 'It's going to be okay, Dad.'"

Lining on bottom of paper

The child, age 8 years, draws her mother and brother to each side of herself and includes the cat. The mother is politically active and oriented to outside family activities. The child draws lines at the bottom of the paper.

V. TREATMENT OF FIGURES: Transparency

This is scored when the child draws: (a) the outline of any figure with clothes drawn around the figure, or (b) an ordinary drawing with the focus on one particular portion of the figure visible through the drawn clothing. If the child draws a baby inside of another figure or internal organs inside of a figure, these are not scored as transparency.

V. TREATMENT OF FIGURES: Missing person or self

This is scored when the child leaves out any living member of the family of origin, including the self. It is important to ask the child if he or she has completed the KFD. Any additions to the KFD after the child has indicated completion should be noted by the clinician and scored as a missing person. Exclusion of deceased family members is not scored as a missing person.

Transparency

A 9-year-old girl shows herself with clothes drawn over her body, which can still be viewed underneath the clothing. The father is shown with transparent pants. In contrast, the brother and mother show no transparency. The girl describes her father with ambivalence. He has molested her repeatedly, but also gives her frequent rewards such as fixing special breakfasts or taking her special places. She describes a situation in which she is treated by her father like a much older woman, "a date." Transparency in this case shows boundaries that have been exceeded, a body that does not quite belong to herself.

Missing person or self

A 15-year-old boy deletes himself from the family. This teen has moved out from the family after his involvement in an auto accident subsequent to drinking and driving. He continues to be a good student and the family agrees to let him live with another family as long as his grades are maintained. Note the space in the drawing. When asked, "Where would you be if you were in this picture?" he pointed to the space and said, "There wasn't enough room to draw myself." He then turned the drawing over amd depicted himself on the back.

V. TREATMENT OF FIGURES: One or more figures drawn on back of paper

This is scored if the child places any family members on the opposite side of the paper from the drawing of the rest of the family.

V. TREATMENT OF FIGURES: Erasures

This is scored if any figure is erased, regardless of whether it is redrawn by the child.

One or more figures drawn on back of paper

A 5-year-old boy draws himself, his sister and his father in a line and puts his stepmother on the back of the page. The father attained child custody and lived alone with the children for many years. The father has just remarried. The boy says, "I wish it was the way it used to be with just the three of us."

Erasures

A 12-year-old boy has had a long history of dental problems and conflicts about the discomfort of dental procedures. In the course of doing the drawing the artist makes many erasures.

V. TREATMENT OF FIGURES: Floating

This is scored if any figure is off the common baseline in a vertical plane 45° in either direction (that is, an upright figure above the baseline). Heads only drawn above the baseline are scored here, if they meet the angle requirement.

V. TREATMENT OF FIGURES: Hanging

This is scored if any figure is depicted as hanging from any object or person. Figures that are depicted by the child as "hanged" should be scored here. Hanging can be depicted as either garroting or dangling from an object.

Floating

A 6-year-old girl draws her father above the clouds, floating. Her father died three months previously. She has just completed a six-week bereavement group for children. Her initial picture showed her father on the baseline with the rest of the family. She now moves him far off the baseline.

Hanging

A young girl, age 9, shows her father hanging the dog from the tree. This is a child caught in the middle of her parents' conflictual divorce. Although the child had personally witnessed several acts of domestic violence by her father toward her mother, the child had also been alienated from her father by the stories she heard from her mother about him. One such story was an incident about the father hanging the family dog from a tree. The child spoke with great emotion about this story, although she did not witness it. The father denied the incident ever happened.

V. TREATMENT OF FIGURES: Falling

This is scored if any figure that is off the common baseline in a vertical plane more than 45° is falling (an upside-down figure). Heads only drawn above the baseline are scored here, if they meet the angle requirement.

V. TREATMENT OF FIGURES: Slanting figures

This is scored if the vertical axis of any figure is tilted by 15° or more. The slanting figure seems to be on the verge of falling over, whether doing an activity or not. Figures that are leaning on some object should be scored here, if the vertical axis of the figure is at a 15° or more angle. (Any figure beyond a 45° angle should be scored as "falling," *not* "slanting.")

Falling

An 8-year-old boy draws a picture of his father pushing him over a ledge of a mountain, unable to break his fall. He writes, "That's me!" His mother and three siblings are shown below. The siblings are shown without faces and the mother is shown with a face looking out and one arm detached from her body, unable to catch him.

This child has endured a long and bitter divorce between the parents in which his father kidnapped him and kept him several months from the mother and other siblings, in spite of her court-ordered custody. Although the boy now lives with his mother, he is court ordered to visit with the father biweekly. The father, an alcoholic, has episodic loss of control and uses excessive discipline with the child. The mother has been unsuccessful in protecting her son from the court-ordered visitations. When the judge saw this picture, he interviewed the child himself and the father was required to complete inpatient treatment before visitation resumed.

Slanting figures

A 6-year-old boy draws his father slanting and above the baseline depicting the unstable situation created when his father decided to separate himself from the family. In this case, the father returned two months later and has stayed with his wife and two sons for many years since.

V. TREATMENT OF FIGURES: Incomplete figures (omission of parts)

This is scored if a figure does not have arms, legs, torso, head, hands or feet. Figures that are depicted as covered by blankets or objects in the foreground of the drawing are not scored as incomplete figures as long as what is seen of the figure has major body parts.

V. TREATMENT OF FIGURES: Extensions/Long legs, arms, equipment

This is scored if a figure has excessively long arms or legs. Exaggeration of limbs to depict motion (e.g., throwing or running) is scored as extensions. Objects on hands or feet that depict rigid extension from the hands or feet may be scored as extensions (e.g., bats, sticks, stilts). These rigid objects must be depicted as being used as an instrument or equipment to be scored as extensions. Flaccid objects held by a figure are not scored as extensions (e.g., balloon or kite strings, ropes, belts, whips).

Incomplete figures (omission of parts)

A child, age 8, deletes arms on herself and her mother whom she describes as "never getting our way." The family adheres to traditional gender roles in which the females feel less powerful. The young girl talked about the conflict between her family's values and her school instruction.

Extensions/Long legs, arms, equipment

An 11-year-old boy described his distress over the competition between his birth father and stepfather. He believed that any positive feeling he had toward the stepfather meant being disloyal to his birth father. Note the long arms on both the child and stepfather. This keeps some distance between himself and his stepfather, even when they are playing.

VI. ACTIONS WITH NEGATIVE ASPECTS: Sexualized
This is scored when overt or subtle sexual activity, dialogue or other sexual content is depicted in the KFD.

A

B

Sexualized

A   The 4-½-year old artist is in the middle in this drawing. He has drawn large explicit genitalia on all three figures. He identifies his brother, age 6, to his right and his father to his left side. Both boys reveal that they have been sexually molested by their father on a recent weekend visitation.

B   Note that this young girl, age 8, has a distorted left arm and emphasizes her breast area. The man in the picture has a zipper with emphasis. The artist reveals, through interview, her incest with her father.

VI. ACTIONS WITH NEGATIVE ASPECTS: Aggression/Weapons

This is scored when overt or subtle aggressive activity, dialogue or other aggressive content is depicted in the KFD. The presence of any obvious weapons or objects used as weapons is scored here. Ambiguous marks described by the child as being weapons are scored here.

VI. ACTIONS WITH NEGATIVE ASPECTS: Fear/Anxiety

This is scored when either or both of the emotions, fear and anxiety, are depicted in the drawing. This is scored if the emotion is conveyed through facial expression, depicted actions, descriptive words or spontaneous environmental additions.

Aggression/Weapons

A   Stark violence depicted by a 10-year-old child living in a war zone of El Salvador. Guns, bullets and bloodshed are shown.

B   A 12-year-old boy draws the "weapon" of the daily injections of insulin experienced in the treatment of his diabetes. Note the negative dialogue: "dummy," "yuk" and "I hate diabetes."

C   A 7-year-old girl referred by child protective services has difficulty verbalizing her dilemma. She draws her mother with a huge stick punishing her and laughing "Ha! ha!" The child feels her mother is getting pleasure from her aggressive act. The words written on the page ensure that the clinician will get the meaning of the picture.

Fear/Anxiety

A   A 5-year-old girl reveals her anxiety about her mother's anger by depicting claws on her mother's distorted long arms. The distortion of the sun impinges upon the face drawn in the picture. History revealed a lack of maternal boundaries and unpredictable violence toward the child.

B   A 12-year-old boy portrays one of 10 hospitalizations. He had a series of surgeries between ages 4–11. In the picture the "jaws" with sharp teeth, to the right and above the child in bed, reveal that a person can draw a smiling face on the child in bed and still use art to express fear of a situation.

VI. ACTIONS WITH NEGATIVE ASPECTS: Withdrawal/Isolation

This is scored when a mood of withdrawal or isolation is depicted in the drawing. This mood may be conveyed by depicted actions, facial expressions, descriptive words or spontaneous environmental additions. Withdrawal/isolation may involve one person or a group of people in the KFD.

VI. ACTIONS WITH NEGATIVE ASPECTS: Blame/Ridicule

This is scored when a mood of blame or ridicule is depicted in the KFD. This mood may be conveyed by depicted actions, facial expressions, descriptive words or spontaneous environmental additions.

Withdrawal/Isolation

A   A child, age 6, shows how isolated the children are from their parents in an otherwise pleasant drawing. The child relates that most of the time her parents do things "by themselves," leaving the children alone to "take care of ourselves."

B   A child, age 9, shows himself leaving his family stating, "I want to run away." His medical diagnosis was diabetes, which he reveals "bugs everyone in the family."

C   A 12-year-old girl reveals herself alone "without a leg to stand on" looking out of the window. Her father had died and she was prevented from going to the funeral with the family. Much of the isolation is depicted in the mood. The view out the window is bleak.

Blame/Ridicule

A 10-year-old girl is very angry at her father's remarriage. She wishes her parents would stay together. From her point of view, her parents would still be married if it weren't for her stepmother. She depicts herself blaming her stepmother who has large arms held behind her back, and a down-turned mouth. The child states that the stepmother can "never do anything right" in the household.

VI. ACTIONS WITH NEGATIVE ASPECTS: Submission/Competition

This is scored if either submission or competition or both are depicted in the drawing. This is scored if it is displayed by facial expression, depicted actions, descriptive words or spontaneous environmental additions. Sporting events may or may not represent competition based on how the child approaches the task (e.g., two children tossing a ball vs. two children racing).

A   B

VI. ACTIONS WITH NEGATIVE ASPECTS: Barriers

This is scored when the child draws an object that provides an impediment between figures. The barrier may be realistic (e.g., a wall) or fanciful (e.g., a large flower). Lines drawn by the child to separate family members would not be scored here (i.e., encapsulations, compartmentalizations). An animal placed between family members is not a barrier if the animal is a family pet. Animals that are not pets should be scored here as barriers (e.g., an elephant).

Submission/Competition

A   A 12-year-old boy feels pressured by his dad to excel at everything he does. Even though the boy can talk honestly with his mother, his father won't listen to her. He draws his overpowering father figure with a large hand, slamming the table. He draws himself as the tiny figure in the foreground. This artist places his mother in the background covering her ears, "afraid to intervene."

B   A 7-year-old year girl depicts the basketball "practice" that occurs at home between her and her mother teamed against her brother and her father. She states: "They always win!"

Barriers

An 8-year-old girl draws two flower barriers at strategic spots, one between her parents on the reader's left side, and one between herself and her younger brother, the second boy from the end on the reader's right. This spontaneous addition depicts areas where problems might exist. There are four children in this family: one girl and three boys. The artist describes her brother, who is one year younger, as, "He gives me the most trouble in the family." The mother recently initiated separation from the father. The barrier between Mom and Dad may depict the recent departure of the mother from the family and the tension that exists between the parents. Note that although both parents are reaching out, they are unable to touch each other. The older son and father's hands are touching, but the only two hands that are holding are those of the artist and her older brother to the reader's left side of the girl. She describes him as the one "I'm closest to."

Interview Guide

The interview guide to kinetic family drawings in Table 10 is constructed like the human figure interview, with questions moving from easiest to more difficult. Note that special effort is taken in the question format to use the third person and impersonal questions such as, "What are good mothers like?" "What are bad mothers like?" "What are good fathers like?" and "What are bad fathers like?"

Children are particularly sensitive to revealing anything negative about either of their parents. They are fully aware of the consequences of such a revelation. To talk in generalities frees communication and usually results in the child revealing his own personal experience. The questions offer a safety net by allowing the child to talk in general terms, so if ever questioned by a parent an "out" is provided. For example, the child can say, "I wasn't talking about you!" In question 12, one would be highly suspicious if the child answered "yes" to both "Is there a secret in your family?" and "Would a kid get in trouble for telling?" Unless the child spontaneously tells the interviewer the secret, however, it is strongly advised that you **do not ask**. Instead, determine whether or not a secret exists and **if** the child would get in trouble for telling it. If an affirmative answer is given, referral may be warranted. This is especially true if there are strong indicators from the drawings, physical findings and other suspicious answers to the interview questions.

Questions 3 and 4 often elicit interesting answers. When a child is asked, "Who do you take after in your family?" the answer is often, "Both of them" (i.e., parents). Question 4, however, "Who do you want to be like when you grow up?" will frequently elicit the person the child has the most respect for or believes to have the most positive personal characteristics.

Note that the last three questions (13, 14, 15) in the KFD interview are similar to those in the HFD interview. Again, these three questions can often be utilized alone in a busy practice to determine whether the full interview is needed. When the interviewer comes to question 15, "Is there anything you don't want me to tell your parents?" it is highly advised that the child's request be honored. When this is not possible (i.e., forensic study), the child should be assured that you will do everything possible to keep the information private, but you cannot promise. The interviewer could state, "If I have to tell, I usually tell it this way. . . . Does that sound okay to you? Can you think of something else I could say that you would like better?" Ideally, the clinician will refer the child to a professional specifically trained to interview traumatized children or follow state requirements, rather than over-reveal information given by the child to anyone, including the parents. It is especially important to continue a supportive, long-term relationship that does not betray a child's trust if one is in the role of the child's physician or teacher.

Continue a supportive, long-term relationship that does not betray the child's trust.

TABLE 10
INTERVIEW GUIDE TO KINETIC FAMILY DRAWINGS

INSTRUCTIONS: Before beginning this interview, determine if the child is in therapy and if so, where in the course of therapy, as this interview may not be applicable. Indicators may be present because the child is "working through" problems.

1. "Let's look at your picture. Tell me who is in your family." (Ask child if it is okay to write names of people below their picture. If not, write on the back of paper or attach paper to recall individuals.)

2. "Do the grown-ups in this family have jobs? What would they be?"

3. "Who do you take after in your family?"

4. "Who do you want to be like when you grow up?"

5. "If a kid needs to make something that was too hard, who would he ask for help in this family?"

6. "Who gives you the hardest time?"

7. "What are good mothers (fathers) like? What are bad mothers (fathers) like?"

8. "All kids do things that make their parents happy or sometimes mad. I sure did. What makes your parents happy? Mad? What happens then?"

9. "What is neat about you? What makes you mad?"

10. "Most families have fights and disagreements. What should they do then?"

11. "If you could have something different about your home what would that be?"

12. "Sometimes families have secrets. Is there a secret in your family? Is the secret a good one or a bad one? Would a kid get in trouble for telling?"

13. "If you had three wishes, what would they be?"

14. "Are things getting better or worse?"

15. "Is there anything you don't want me to tell your parents?"

FIGURE 9: THE "PERFECT FAMILY" WITH STRESS ART INDICATORS
(See scoring inventory on page 108.)

Chapter 5

Implications of Systematic Screening for Child Art Indicators

Using this screening tool, it is now possible to enable a child to communicate his or her most intimate and difficult experiences, namely, emotional and physical trauma. Children can be screened for physical, emotional or sexual abuse using drawings as the communicating medium. For those working with children, this tool provides a means to gather reliable and valid data about the child's life experiences. The screening inventory gives the clinician information that would otherwise be difficult, if not impossible, to obtain.

In general, people possess a natural tendency to flee from situations that frighten them without declaring their hidden stress. Children are no exception. The drawings of traumatized children often have the themes of "the perfect family" or "putting on a happy face" even though the child and family may be enduring extremely stressful circumstances. At a casual glance, a drawing may be judged as "normal, happy or joyous." A person educated in drawing interpretation may, however, find indicators of underlying stress. Note that the drawing in Figure 9, by the daughter of a medical student, has all the emotional characteristics of joy, but also has many quantitative indicators of the stress imposed by the father's educational priority (see authors' scoring of drawing, page 108).

Children, like adults, often cannot find the words to communicate their feelings or describe situations or experiences. The example above illustrates how drawing bridges a communication barrier. The nonthreatening nature of drawing allows a child to easily reveal indicators that can be interpreted to normal but stressed parents, who can then make family adjustments. In addition, the screening tool provides an indelible picture to compare the child's perceptions by requesting another drawing once family changes are made.

In some cases, the interview alone is perfectly adequate to establish child circumstances, but it can be enhanced by the production of a picture. One of the authors (M.H.) interviewed a 9-year-old boy to determine whether the child's mother was exposing him to drugs during his court-ordered visitation. The following conversation ensued:

M.H.: Tell me about anything you might have noticed about your Mom or the people she lives with using drugs.

Child: She didn't do drugs, but the people around her did.

M.H.: How did you know?

Child: They had a tube and it went into a bowl and they were blowing bubbles into it and it made noise . . . like when you slurp up the last bit of soda from a glass.

While relating this "word picture," the boy was also noticeably wrinkling up his face as if smelling the drugs he was describing. This child's description is authentically detailed and one can envision a picture of the scene in one's own mind. Asking the child to draw the scene allows communication to a wider audience (the court) and keeps the work intact for filing.

The most difficult step in implementing this method of screening is the interpretation of drawings. It is important to maintain objectivity and to avoid subjective tendencies. It is perfectly all right to ask the child, "What is this?" or "If this part of your picture could talk, what would it say?" It is important to use the child's explanation, not the clinician's. A clinician might interpret a drawing of the sun to mean either that the child is physically warm or that the child needs emotional warmth. The depiction of rain or clouds in a picture may seem gloomy or comforting to the clinician. It is important to resist projecting one's adult interpretation onto the drawing. The clinician should simply accept the drawing without interpreting it or with the child's spontaneous interpretation as, for example, "It's a sad picture." In addition, once a child has drawn an indicator such as clouds, it is important for the clinician to avoid inadvertently "prompting" the child toward making additions to his picture by talking out loud about it. One of the authors (L.W.P.) commented to a bereaved child, "I notice you drew clouds in your picture." Immediately the child, who was experiencing grief about his recently departed father, drew in a bright yellow sun in the left side of his picture changing his authentic original work. When something is obvious to the viewer (such as clouds), the less said, the better.

This screening method stresses standardized steps to review drawings and maintain reliability and validity. Left with a child's drawing in hand, a clinician is less apt to "forget" what the child is trying to communicate. Looking at a drawing later may also evoke a new understanding, which is not evident in the immediacy of the clinical situation.

The implications of the drawing method go beyond the personal and familial. The following case shows how the directness of a child's drawing can help the wider community.

A 10-year-old daughter of a bombing suspect made crayon drawings of dynamite, wires and other parts of a box she saw her father and his friend build. The child stopped short of calling the project a "bomb," but her drawings included the components of the bomb that exploded, permanently blinding and disabling a state trooper when he opened his mailbox. "I heard them say it was some sort of present," the child witnessed to the district attorney. Cross examination of this child, using the drawing during the court proceedings, was the key to the conviction of this suspect (Reno Gazette-Journal, 1994).

Hewitt and Arrowood (1994) devised a systematic touch continuum procedure for young children, utilizing a directed drawing task with a clinical interview. Results of their pilot study revealed an effective method for screening children for potential physical or sexual abuse. The systematic touch continuum procedure has been successfully admitted in court cases in Minnesota as an appropriate screening format. This innovative technique is not perfect, yielding a "bias toward children underreporting" when actual abuse had occurred. The authors suggest that the use of the screening techniques for HFDs and KFDs described in this book in combination with the systematic touch continuum procedure may be an effective and comprehensive assessment for forensic purposes.

With time, the use of drawings in forensic proceedings will certainly increase. Now that a standardized method to collect and interpret children's drawings is available, concerned persons working with children can investigate suspicious adult behavior and perhaps discover the cause of the child's stress or traumatic experiences. Stress can be there whether it is directed toward or witnessed by the child. If one only cares to look, one can find what a child is "telling without telling."

SCREENING INVENTORY FOR KINETIC FAMILY DRAWING

Scoring of "Perfect Family" Drawing by Authors

Name: _____Jane_____   Date: __9/3/93__   Age: __5-1/2__

	RED FLAGS	YELLOW FLAGS	GREEN FLAGS

Qualitative

I. QUALITY OF OVERALL DRAWING

		RED FLAGS	YELLOW FLAGS	GREEN FLAGS
1)	Peculiarity/Strangeness	☐ Very peculiar	☑ Somewhat peculiar	☐ Not at all peculiar
2)	Feeling/Mood	☐ Depressed/Angry	☐ Mixed emotions	☑ Happy/Content
3)	Order	☐ Unorganized	☐ Partially organized	☑ Orderly

II. CHILD PERCEPTION OF FAMILY MEMBERS

1)	Size	☐ Very disproportionate	☐ Some disproportion	☑ Proportionate
2)	Shape	☐ Very disproportionate	☑ Some disproportion	☐ Proportionate
3)	Distortion	☐ Excessive	☑ Some	☐ None

III. CHILD SELF-PERCEPTION IN FAMILY SYSTEM

1)	Size	☐ Very disproportionate	☐ Some disproportion	☑ Proportionate
2)	Shape	☐ Very disproportionate	☑ Some disproportion	☐ Proportionate
3)	Distortion	☐ Excessive	☑ Some	☐ None

Because of the complexity of the KFD and the lack of quantification for peculiarity and order, always interview the child if the drawing shows excessive disorder (chaos) or peculiarity, as these are not factored in the scoring system.

Quantitative

IV. STYLES (Note which figure on dotted line)

1)	Encapsulation	(Present (2.0))	Self, female above star	Absent (0)
2)	Compartmentalization	(Present (2.0))	Four figures at corners	Absent (0)
3)	Writing words on picture	Present (1.0)		Absent (0)
4)	Edging	Present (1.0)		Absent (0)
5)	Underlining individual figures	(Present (0.5))	Top left figure	Absent (0)
6)	Lining at top of paper	Present (0.5)		Absent (0)
7)	Lining at bottom of paper	Present (0.5)		Absent (0)

V. TREATMENT OF FIGURES (Note which figure on dotted line)

1)	Transparency	(Present (2.0))	Female figure above star	Absent (0)
2)	Missing person or self	Present (2.0)		Absent (0)
3)	One or more figures drawn on back of paper	Present (1.0)		Absent (0)
4)	Erasures	Present (1.0)		Absent (0)
5)	Floating	(Present (1.0))	Top right figure	Absent (0)
6)	Hanging	Present (1.0)		Absent (0)
7)	Falling	Present (0.5)		Absent (0)
8)	Slanting figures	Present (0.5)		Absent (0)
9)	Incomplete figures (omission of parts)	(Present (0.5))	Heads on bottom row	Absent (0)
10)	Extensions/Long legs, arms, equipment	(Present (0.5))	Top right figure	Absent (0)

VI. ACTIONS WITH NEGATIVE ASPECTS (Note which figure on dotted line)

1)	Sexualized	Present (2.0)		Absent (0)
2)	Aggression/Weapons	Present (2.0)		Absent (0)
3)	Fear/Anxiety	Present (2.0)		Absent (0)
4)	Withdrawal/Isolation	(Present (1.0))	Self and female figure above star	Absent (0)
5)	Blame/Ridicule	Present (1.0)		Absent (0)
6)	Submission/Competition	Present (0.5)		Absent (0)
7)	Barriers	Present (0.5)		Absent (0)

☐ Normal (0-2)   ☐ Undetermined (3-5)   ☑ Suspicious/Refer (6+)   **TOTAL OVERALL SCORE: 9.5**

Notes _____

These results are NOT diagnostic for physical, sexual or emotional abuse. The results provide CLUES for the clinician for further investigation by child interview, physical exam and forensic evaluation.

© 1995 Peterson/Hardin
(Adapted from Burns & Kaufman, 1972)

Afterword

Although this book has a quantitative orientation, its purpose is to emphasize the importance of the child's truth as it is communicated by the child. When the child's drawing speaks of trauma, it must be accepted as the truth, in this or an alternative reality, rather than as the imagination of the child. We hope this work lends credence to the child, so that he will be honored and respected for his perception.

The authors suggest, however, that drawings be only one piece of evidence in the context of collaborating evidence. We find it helpful to organize our collection of data around the known symptoms of childhood posttraumatic stress disorder. We ask historical questions to determine if there has been a sudden change in behavior, including acting out or withdrawal from specific persons, places or things. We assess if there are specific fears that are trauma related. We determine if the child has re-enacted the trauma with dolls, or on other children and adults. We check on the recent occurrence of nightmares or changes in eating, sleeping or dreaming patterns. We ask about the presence of any headaches or stomachaches. From the physical exam we look for suspicious bruises, mouth sores, or reddening in the groin, belly or genital area. Unusual posturing is noted, such as arching the back when placed on hands and knees for evaluation of the anal area, as has been seen in sodomized children. When the confirming data is collected, we advise following state regulations by reporting to child protective services.

Children have a strong need for control and want to express their own point of view rather than the views of their adult caretakers. Art cannot be "coached"— it is a natural expression that has no rules of conformity. Children need to be in control of their own way of expression, their environment and their color choices. Providing a wide range of art materials and colored pencils without intrusion ultimately facilitates the greatest expression and healing.

We have minimized the use of color in our discussion of the diagnostic aspects of children's artwork, although it is repeatedly debated among ourselves. While we agree that the people and objects drawn depict the content of trauma, we speculate that color choices depict feelings for children. Furthermore, the intensity and placement of color may suggest the level of trauma held within the child. The exploration and interpretation of color is the next leading edge for those who wish not only to diagnose but also to participate in life as it is seen through the child's eyes.

Once one has the ability to see the world as it is seen by the child, one is faced with the problem of how to interpret this world to the child's significant adult caretakers, who will often say, "This has nothing to do with reality." What seems imperative to us as clinicians is to have the courage to reply, "This is how this child perceives it, and that makes it real—real enough to affect behavior, beliefs and feelings."

"NORMAL" HUMAN FIGURE DRAWING

Self-Test 1

● Omission of genital area ● Encapsulation ● Extensions
● Hearts ● Jagged teeth ● Poor integration of body parts

SCREENING INVENTORY FOR
CHILD HUMAN FIGURE DRAWING
Self-Test 1

Name: __Ron__   Date: __2/14/91__   Age: __9__

1.	**Explicit drawing of genitalia**	Present (3.0)	Absent (0)
2.	**Concealment of genitalia**	Present (3.0)	Absent (0)
3.	**Omission of genital area**	(Present (3.0))	Absent (0)
4.	**Omission of central part of figure**	Present (3.0)	Absent (0)
5.	**Encapsulation**	(Present (3.0))	Absent (0)
6.	**Fruit trees added**	Present (3.0)	Absent (0)
7.	**Opposite sex drawn**	Present (3.0)	Absent (0)
8.	Tiny figure	Present (2.0)	Absent (0)
9.	Poor integration of body parts/ Monster drawn	(Present (2.0))	Absent (0)
10.	Hands cut off	Present (2.0)	Absent (0)
11.	Omission of peripheral body parts (arms or legs)	Present (2.0)	Absent (0)
12.	Belly button added or emphasized	Present (2.0)	Absent (0)
13.	Jagged teeth	(Present (2.0))	Absent (0)
14.	Big hands	Present (2.0)	Absent (0)
15.	Transparency	Present (2.0)	Absent (0)
16.	Slanting figure	Present (1.0)	Absent (0)
17.	Genitals emphasized	Present (1.0)	Absent (0)
18.	Legs tightly together	Present (1.0)	Absent (0)
19.	Waist cut off	Present (1.0)	Absent (0)
20.	Extensions/Long arms/Long legs	(Present (1.0))	Absent (0)
21.	Rainbows	Present (0.5)	Absent (0)
22.	Butterflies	Present (0.5)	Absent (0)
23.	Hearts	(Present (0.5))	Absent (0)
24.	Flying birds	Present (0.5)	Absent (0)
25.	Rain/Clouds	Present (0.5)	Absent (0)
26.	Shading of face	Present (0.5)	Absent (0)
27.	Unicorns	Present (0.5)	Absent (0)
28.	X for eyes	Present (0.5)	Absent (0)

Total Overall Score _____11.5_____

Scoring for this drawing: (check one)   ❑ **Normal (0-2)**   ❑ **Undetermined (3-5)**   ☑ **Suspicious/Refer (6+)**

Notes _____
_____
_____

These results are NOT diagnostic for physical, sexual or emotional abuse. The results provide CLUES   © 1995 Hardin/Peterson
for the clinician for further investigation by child interview, physical exam and forensic evaluation.

Self-Test 2

SCREENING INVENTORY FOR
CHILD HUMAN FIGURE DRAWING
Self-Test 2

Name: **Danika**   Date: **3/15/94**   Age: **10**

1. **Explicit drawing of genitalia**   Present (3.0) ....Absent (0)
2. **Concealment of genitalia**   Present (3.0) ....Absent (0)
3. **Omission of genital area**   Present (3.0) ....Absent (0)
4. **Omission of central part of figure**   Present (3.0) ....Absent (0)
5. **Encapsulation**   (Present (3.0)) ....Absent (0)
6. **Fruit trees added**   (Present (3.0)) ....Absent (0)
7. **Opposite sex drawn**   Present (3.0) ....Absent (0)
8. Tiny figure   Present (2.0) ....Absent (0)
9. Poor integration of body parts/
   Monster drawn   Present (2.0) ....Absent (0)
10. Hands cut off   Present (2.0) ....Absent (0)
11. Omission of peripheral body parts
    (arms or legs)   Present (2.0) ....Absent (0)
12. Belly button added or emphasized   Present (2.0) ....Absent (0)
13. Jagged teeth   Present (2.0) ....Absent (0)
14. Big hands   Present (2.0) ....Absent (0)
15. Transparency   Present (2.0) ....Absent (0)
16. Slanting figure   Present (1.0) ....Absent (0)
17. Genitals emphasized   Present (1.0) ....Absent (0)
18. Legs tightly together   Present (1.0) ....Absent (0)
19. Waist cut off   Present (1.0) ....Absent (0)
20. Extensions/Long arms/Long legs   Present (1.0) ....Absent (0)
21. Rainbows   Present (0.5) ....Absent (0)
22. Butterflies   Present (0.5) ....Absent (0)
23. Hearts   Present (0.5) ....Absent (0)
24. Flying birds   Present (0.5) ....Absent (0)
25. Rain/Clouds   Present (0.5) ....Absent (0)
26. Shading of face   Present (0.5) ....Absent (0)
27. Unicorns   (Present (0.5)) ....Absent (0)
28. X for eyes   Present (0.5) ....Absent (0)

Total Overall Score _____ 6.5 _____

Scoring for this drawing: (check one)   ❏ Normal (0-2)   ❏ Undetermined (3-5)   ☑ Suspicious/Refer (6+)

Notes _____

These results are NOT diagnostic for physical, sexual or emotional abuse. The results provide CLUES   © 1995 Hardin/Peterson
for the clinician for further investigation by child interview, physical exam and forensic evaluation.

Self-Test 3

Concealment of genitalia • Encapsulation • Slanting Figure • Hearts

SCREENING INVENTORY FOR
CHILD HUMAN FIGURE DRAWING
Self-Test 3

Name: **Dorothy** _____   Date: **4/22/93** _____   Age: **7** _____

1.	**Explicit drawing of genitalia**	Present (3.0)	Absent (0)
2.	**Concealment of genitalia**	(Present (3.0))	Absent (0)
3.	**Omission of genital area**	Present (3.0)	Absent (0)
4.	**Omission of central part of figure**	Present (3.0)	Absent (0)
5.	**Encapsulation**	(Present (3.0))	Absent (0)
6.	**Fruit trees added**	Present (3.0)	Absent (0)
7.	**Opposite sex drawn**	Present (3.0)	Absent (0)
8.	Tiny figure	Present (2.0)	Absent (0)
9.	Poor integration of body parts/ Monster drawn	Present (2.0)	Absent (0)
10.	Hands cut off	Present (2.0)	Absent (0)
11.	Omission of peripheral body parts (arms or legs)	Present (2.0)	Absent (0)
12.	Belly button added or emphasized	Present (2.0)	Absent (0)
13.	Jagged teeth	Present (2.0)	Absent (0)
14.	Big hands	Present (2.0)	Absent (0)
15.	Transparency	Present (2.0)	Absent (0)
16.	Slanting figure	(Present (1.0))	Absent (0)
17.	Genitals emphasized	Present (1.0)	Absent (0)
18.	Legs tightly together	Present (1.0)	Absent (0)
19.	Waist cut off	Present (1.0)	Absent (0)
20.	Extensions/Long arms/Long legs	Present (1.0)	Absent (0)
21.	Rainbows	Present (0.5)	Absent (0)
22.	Butterflies	Present (0.5)	Absent (0)
23.	Hearts	(Present (0.5))	Absent (0)
24.	Flying birds	Present (0.5)	Absent (0)
25.	Rain/Clouds	Present (0.5)	Absent (0)
26.	Shading of face	Present (0.5)	Absent (0)
27.	Unicorns	Present (0.5)	Absent (0)
28.	X for eyes	Present (0.5)	Absent (0)

Total Overall Score _____ **7.5** _____

Scoring for this drawing: (check one)   ❑ **Normal (0-2)**   ❑ **Undetermined (3-5)**   ☑ **Suspicious/Refer (6+)**

Notes _____
_____
_____

These results are NOT diagnostic for physical, sexual or emotional abuse. The results provide CLUES for the clinician for further investigation by child interview, physical exam and forensic evaluation.   © 1995 Hardin/Peterson

"NORMAL" KINETIC FAMILY DRAWING

Self-Test 4

Child, age 9, drew this KFD of his parents. Mother is in the foreground.
Father, in the background. The child eliminated himself.

SCREENING INVENTORY FOR KINETIC FAMILY DRAWING
Self-Test 4

Name: __Michael__   Date: __6/30/90__   Age: __9__

	RED FLAGS	YELLOW FLAGS	GREEN FLAGS

Qualitative

I.   QUALITY OF OVERALL DRAWING
1) Peculiarity/Strangeness — ☑ Very peculiar ☐ Somewhat peculiar ☐ Not at all peculiar
2) Feeling/Mood — ☐ Depressed/Angry ☑ Mixed emotions ☐ Happy/Content
3) Order — ☐ Unorganized ☑ Partially organized ☐ Orderly

II. CHILD PERCEPTION OF FAMILY MEMBERS
1) Size — ☑ Very disproportionate ☐ Some disproportion ☐ Proportionate
2) Shape — ☑ Very disproportionate ☐ Some disproportion ☐ Proportionate
3) Distortion — ☑ Excessive ☐ Some ☐ None

III. CHILD SELF-PERCEPTION IN FAMILY SYSTEM   (Self deleted)
1) Size — ☐ Very disproportionate ☐ Some disproportion ☐ Proportionate
2) Shape — ☐ Very disproportionate ☐ Some disproportion ☐ Proportionate
3) Distortion — ☐ Excessive ☐ Some ☐ None

Because of the complexity of the KFD and the lack of quantification for peculiarity and order, always interview the child if the drawing shows excessive disorder (chaos) or peculiarity, as these are not factored in the scoring system.

Quantitative

IV. STYLES (Note which figure on dotted line)
1) Encapsulation .... Present (2.0) .... Absent (0)
2) Compartmentalization .... Present (2.0) .... Absent (0)
3) Writing words on picture .... Present (1.0) .... Absent (0)
4) Edging .... Present (1.0) .... Absent (0)
5) Underlining individual figures ..... (Present (0.5)) .... Mother .... Absent (0)
6) Lining at top of paper .... Present (0.5) .... Absent (0)
7) Lining at bottom of paper .... Present (0.5) .... Absent (0)

V.   TREATMENT OF FIGURES (Note which figure on dotted line)
1) Transparency .... (Present (2.0)) .... Mother .... Absent (0)
2) Missing person or self .... (Present (2.0)) .... Self .... Absent (0)
3) One or more figures drawn
   on back of paper .... Present (1.0) .... Absent (0)
4) Erasures .... Present (1.0) .... Absent (0)
5) Floating .... (Present (1.0)) .... Father .... Absent (0)
6) Hanging .... Present (1.0) .... Absent (0)
7) Falling .... Present (0.5) .... Absent (0)
8) Slanting figures .... (Present (0.5)) .... Mother .... Absent (0)
9) Incomplete figures (omission of parts) Present (0.5) .... Absent (0)
10) Extensions/Long legs, arms, equipment (Present (0.5)) ... Father, Mother .... Absent (0)

VI. ACTIONS WITH NEGATIVE ASPECTS (Note which figure on dotted line)
1) Sexualized .... Present (2.0) .... Absent (0)
2) Aggression/Weapons .... (Present (2.0)) .... Father .... Absent (0)
3) Fear/Anxiety .... Present (2.0) .... Absent (0)
4) Withdrawal/Isolation .... Present (1.0) .... Absent (0)
5) Blame/Ridicule .... Present (1.0) .... Absent (0)
6) Submission/Competition .... Present (0.5) .... Absent (0)
7) Barriers .... Present (0.5) .... Absent (0)

☐ Normal (0-2)   ☐ Undetermined (3-5)   ☑ Suspicious/Refer (6+)   **TOTAL OVERALL SCORE:** __8.5__

Notes _____

These results are NOT diagnostic for physical, sexual or emotional abuse. The results provide CLUES for the clinician for further investigation by child interview, physical exam and forensic evaluation.

© 1995 Peterson/Hardin
(Adapted from Burns & Kaufman, 1972)

Self-Test 5

A 7-year-old girl draws her family. Left to right: older brother playing soccer with the artist; Father hanging the family dog; Mother watering flowers.

SCREENING INVENTORY FOR KINETIC FAMILY DRAWING
Self-Test 5

Name: **Susan**   Date: **6/1/91**   Age: **7**

	RED FLAGS	**YELLOW FLAGS**	**GREEN FLAGS**

Qualitative

I.   QUALITY OF OVERALL DRAWING
1) Peculiarity/Strangeness — ☐ Very peculiar — ☑ Somewhat peculiar — ☐ Not at all peculiar
2) Feeling/Mood — ☐ Depressed/Angry — ☑ Mixed emotions — ☐ Happy/Content
3) Order — ☐ Unorganized — ☐ Partially organized — ☑ Orderly

II.   CHILD PERCEPTION OF FAMILY MEMBERS
1) Size — ☑ Very disproportionate — ☐ Some disproportion — ☐ Proportionate
2) Shape — ☐ Very disproportionate — ☐ Some disproportion — ☑ Proportionate
3) Distortion — ☐ Excessive — ☑ Some — ☐ None

III. CHILD SELF-PERCEPTION IN FAMILY SYSTEM
1) Size — ☐ Very disproportionate — ☑ Some disproportion — ☐ Proportionate
2) Shape — ☐ Very disproportionate — ☑ Some disproportion — ☐ Proportionate
3) Distortion — ☐ Excessive — ☐ Some — ☑ None

Because of the complexity of the KFD and the lack of quantification for peculiarity and order, always interview the child if the drawing shows excessive disorder (chaos) or peculiarity, as these are not factored in the scoring system.

Quantitative

IV.   STYLES (Note which figure on dotted line)
1) Encapsulation — (Present (2.0)) ... Father (by tree and dog) ... Absent (0)
2) Compartmentalization — (Present (2.0)) ... Self ... Absent (0)
3) Writing words on picture — Present (1.0) ... Absent (0)
4) Edging — Present (1.0) ... Absent (0)
5) Underlining individual figures — Present (0.5) ... Absent (0)
6) Lining at top of paper — Present (0.5) ... Absent (0)
7) Lining at bottom of paper — Present (0.5) ... Absent (0)

V.   TREATMENT OF FIGURES (Note which figure on dotted line)
1) Transparency — Present (2.0) ... Absent (0)
2) Missing person or self — Present (2.0) ... Absent (0)
3) One or more figures drawn on back of paper — Present (1.0) ... Absent (0)
4) Erasures — Present (1.0) ... Absent (0)
5) Floating — (Present (1.0)) ... Older brother ... Absent (0)
6) Hanging — (Present (1.0)) ... Pet dog ... Absent (0)
7) Falling — Present (0.5) ... Absent (0)
8) Slanting figures — Present (0.5) ... Absent (0)
9) Incomplete figures (omission of parts) — Present (0.5) ... Absent (0)
10) Extensions/Long legs, arms, equipment — (Present (0.5)) ... Mother ... Absent (0)

VI.   ACTIONS WITH NEGATIVE ASPECTS (Note which figure on dotted line)
1) Sexualized — Present (2.0) ... Absent (0)
2) Aggression/Weapons — (Present (2.0)) ... Father ... Absent (0)
3) Fear/Anxiety — Present (2.0) ... Absent (0)
4) Withdrawal/Isolation — Present (1.0) ... Absent (0)
5) Blame/Ridicule — Present (1.0) ... Absent (0)
6) Submission/Competition — Present (0.5) ... Absent (0)
7) Barriers — (Present (0.5)) ... Tree ... Absent (0)

☐ Normal (0-2)   ☐ Undetermined (3-5)   ☑ Suspicious/Refer (6+)   **TOTAL OVERALL SCORE:** __9__

Notes _____

These results are NOT diagnostic for physical, sexual or emotional abuse. The results provide CLUES for the clinician for further investigation by child interview, physical exam and forensic evaluation.

© 1995 Peterson/Hardin
(Adapted from Burns & Kaufman, 1972)

Self-Test 6

An 8-year-old girl drew her family and labeled each member.
The partially completed figure in the lower center portion
was originally intended to be the Father, according to the child.

SCREENING INVENTORY FOR KINETIC FAMILY DRAWING
Self-Test 6

Name: **Renne**   Date: **9/28/93**   Age: **8**

	RED FLAGS	YELLOW FLAGS	GREEN FLAGS

Qualitative

I. QUALITY OF OVERALL DRAWING

		RED FLAGS	YELLOW FLAGS	GREEN FLAGS
1)	Peculiarity/Strangeness	☑ Very peculiar	☐ Somewhat peculiar	☐ Not at all peculiar
2)	Feeling/Mood	☐ Depressed/Angry	☑ Mixed emotions	☐ Happy/Content
3)	Order	☐ Unorganized	☑ Partially organized	☐ Orderly

II. CHILD PERCEPTION OF FAMILY MEMBERS

1)	Size	☐ Very disproportionate	☐ Some disproportion	☑ Proportionate
2)	Shape	☐ Very disproportionate	☐ Some disproportion	☑ Proportionate
3)	Distortion	☐ Excessive	☑ Some	☐ None

III. CHILD SELF-PERCEPTION IN FAMILY SYSTEM

1)	Size	☐ Very disproportionate	☐ Some disproportion	☑ Proportionate
2)	Shape	☐ Very disproportionate	☑ Some disproportion	☐ Proportionate
3)	Distortion	☐ Excessive	☐ Some	☑ None

Because of the complexity of the KFD and the lack of quantification for peculiarity and order, always interview the child if the drawing shows excessive disorder (chaos) or peculiarity, as these are not factored in the scoring system.

Quantitative

IV. STYLES (Note which figure on dotted line)

1)	Encapsulation	Present (2.0)	Absent (0)
2)	Compartmentalization	Present (2.0)	Absent (0)
3)	Writing words on picture	Present (1.0)	Absent (0)
4)	Edging	Present (1.0)	Absent (0)
5)	Underlining individual figures	Present (0.5)	Absent (0)
6)	Lining at top of paper	Present (0.5)	Absent (0)
7)	Lining at bottom of paper	Present (0.5)	Absent (0)

V. TREATMENT OF FIGURES (Note which figure on dotted line)

1)	Transparency	(Present (2.0)) .... Self	Absent (0)
2)	Missing person or self	Present (2.0)	Absent (0)
3)	One or more figures drawn on back of paper	Present (1.0)	Absent (0)
4)	Erasures	Present (1.0)	Absent (0)
5)	Floating	(Present (1.0)) .... All	Absent (0)
6)	Hanging	Present (1.0)	Absent (0)
7)	Falling	Present (0.5)	Absent (0)
8)	Slanting figures	(Present (0.5)) .... Dad	Absent (0)
9)	Incomplete figures (omission of parts)	(Present (0.5)) .... Joey and self	Absent (0)
10)	Extensions/Long legs, arms, equipment	Present (0.5)	Absent (0)

VI. ACTIONS WITH NEGATIVE ASPECTS (Note which figure on dotted line)

1)	Sexualized	Present (2.0)	Absent (0)
2)	Aggression/Weapons	Present (2.0)	Absent (0)
3)	Fear/Anxiety	Present (2.0)	Absent (0)
4)	Withdrawal/Isolation	Present (1.0)	Absent (0)
5)	Blame/Ridicule	Present (1.0)	Absent (0)
6)	Submission/Competition	Present (0.5)	Absent (0)
7)	Barriers	Present (0.5)	Absent (0)

☐ Normal (0-2)   ☑ Undetermined (3-5)   ☐ Suspicious/Refer (6+)   **TOTAL OVERALL SCORE:** ___4___

Notes _____

These results are NOT diagnostic for physical, sexual or emotional abuse. The results provide CLUES for the clinician for further investigation by child interview, physical exam and forensic evaluation.

© 1995 Peterson/Hardin
(Adapted from Burns & Kaufman, 1972)

References

Achterberg J. and Lawlis, G. *Imagery and disease.* Champaign, Illinois: Institute for Personality and Ability Testing, 1984.

Achterberg J. *Imagery and healing.* Berkeley, CA: Shambala, 1985.

Altschuler RH. and Hattwick LW. *Paintings and personality: A study of young children.* (2 volumes). Chicago: University of Chicago Press, 1947.

Ards S. and Harrell A. Reporting of child maltreatment: a secondary analysis of the National Incidence Surveys. *Child Abuse and Neglect* l993; 17:337-44.

Baccino E., de Saint Martin Pernot L. and Gaccardy-Androuin C. Child sexual abuse and physicians: The 1992 Finestere (France) Study. *Journal of Clinical Forensic Medicine,* 2, 1995.

Baldwin DC. The effect of dental extraction upon the size of human figure drawings. *Journal of Dental Research,* 43, 826, 1964.

Bell JE. *Projective techniques: A dynamic approach to the study of personality.* New York: Longmans, Green and Co., 1948.

Browne A., and Finkelhor D. Impact of child sexual abuse: A review of the research. *Psychological Bulletin,* 99, 66-77, 1986.

Buck JN. The H-T-P test. *Journal of Clinical Psychology,* 4, 151-159, 1948a.

Buck JN. The H-T-P technique: A qualitative and quantitative scoring manual. *Journal of Clinical Psychology,* 4, 317-396, 1948b.

Burgess AW., Hartman CR., McCausland MP., and Powers P. Response patterns in children and adolescents exploited through sex rings and pornography. *American Journal of Psychiatry,* 141, 656-662, 1984.

Burns RC. and Kaufman SH. *Kinetic family drawings.* New York: Brunner/Mazel, 1970.

Burns RC. and Kaufman SH. *Actions, styles and symbols in kinetic family drawings (K-F-D): An interpretative manual,* New York: Brunner/Mazel, 1972.

Coles R. *Their eyes meeting the world: The drawings and paintings of children.* Boston: Houghton Mifflin Co., 1992.

Cox M. and Parkin C. Young children's human figure drawing: Cross-sectional and longitudinal studies. *Educational Psychology,* 6, 353-368, l986.

Cox M. *Children's drawings of the human figure.* Hillsdale, USA: Lawrence Erlbaum Associates, 1993.

Court E. Drawing on culture: The influence of culture on children's drawing performance in rural Kenya. *Journal of Art and Design Education,* 8, 65-88, l989.

Dennis W. *Group values through children's drawings.* New York: Wiley, 1964.

De Francis V. *Protecting the child victim of sex crimes committed by adults.* Denver: American Humane Association, 1969.

DiLeo JH. *Young children and their drawings.* New York: Brunner/Mazel, 1970.

DiLeo JH. *Children's drawings as diagnostic aids.* New York: Brunner/Mazel, 1973.

DiLeo JH. *Child development: Analysis and synthesis.* New York: Brunner/Mazel, 1977.

DiLeo JH. *Interpreting children's drawings.* New York: Brunner/Mazel, 1983.

Dillard HK. and Landsman M. The Evanston Early Identification Scales: Prediction of school problems from the human figure drawings of kindergarten children. *Journal of Clinical Psychology,* 24, 227-228, 1968.

Elliot A. and Peterson L. Maternal sexual abuse of male children: When to suspect and how to uncover it. *Postgraduate Medicine,* 94, 169-180, 1993.

Everstein DS. and Everstein L. *Sexual trauma in children and adolescents: Dynamics and treatments,* New York: Brunner/Mazel, 1989.

Faller KC. Is the child victim of sexual abuse telling the truth? *Child Abuse and Neglect,* 8, 473-481, 1984.

Feldman W., Feldman E., Goodman JT. and McGrath PJ. Is childhood sexual abuse really increasing in prevalence? An analysis of the evidence. *Pediatrics,* 88, 29-33, 1991.

Finkelhor D. and Dziuba-Leatherman J. Victimization of children. *American Psychologist,* 49, l73-183, l994.

Fortes M. Children's drawings among the Tallensi. *Africa,* 13, 239-295, l940.

Fortes M. Tallensi children's drawings. In B. Lloyd and J. Gay (Eds.), *Universals of human thought.* Cambridge: Cambridge University Press, l981.

Frankenburg, W. *Denver 11.* Denver: Denver Developmental Material, l990.

Frankenburg WK., Dodds JB. and Fandal AW. *Denver Developmental Screening Test: Manual/workbook for nursing and paramedical personnel.* Denver: Ladoca, l973.

Furth GM. *The secret world of drawings: Healing through art.* Boston: Sigo Press, 1988.

Gesell A. *The mental growth of the pre-school child.* New York: Macmillan, l925.

Goodenough F. *Measurement of intelligence by drawing.* Yonkers, NY: World Book, 1926.

Goodenough FL. Studies in the psychology of children's drawings. *Psychological Bulletin,* 25, 272-283, 1928.

Goodwin J. Use of drawings in evaluating children who may be incest victims. *Children and Youth Services Review,* 4, 269-278, l982.

Hulse WC. The emotionally disturbed child draws his family. *Quarterly Journal of Child Behavior,* 3, 152, 1951.

Hammer EF. Guide for qualitative research with the H-T-P. *Journal of General Psychology,* 51, 41-60, 1960.

Hardin M. Unpublished dissertation, University of Nevada, 1989.

Harris DB. *Children's drawings as measures of intellectual maturity: A revision and extension of the Goodenough Draw-A-Man Test.* New York: Harcourt, Brace and World, l963.

Hewitt SK. and Arrowood AA. Systematic touch exploration as a screening procedure for child abuse: A pilot study. *Journal of Child Sexual Abuse,* 3(2), 31-41, 1994.

Hibbard R. and Foghmann K. Genitalia in children's drawing: An association with sexual abuse. *Pediatrics,* 79, 129-136, 1987.

Jolles I. *A catalog for the qualitative interpretation of the H-T-P.* Los Angeles: Western Psychological Services, 1971.

Kaufman B. and Wohl A. *Casualities of childhood a developmental perspective in sexual abuse using projective drawings.* New York: Brunner/Mazel, 1992.

Kempe RS. and Kempe CH. *The common secret: Sexual abuse of children and adolescents.* New York: Freeman and Company, 1984.

Kessler DB. and Hyden P. Physical, sexual, and emotional abuse of children. *Clinical Symposia,* 43, 1-32, 1991.

Klepsch M. and Logie L. *Children draw and tell: An introduction to the projective uses of children's human figure drawings.* New York: Brunner/Mazel, 1982.

Koppitz EM. Emotional indicators on human figure drawings of children: A validation study. *Journal of Clinical Psychology,* 22, 466-469, 1966a.

Koppitz EM. Emotional indicators on human figure drawings and school achievement of first and second grades. *Journal of Clinical Psychology,* 22, 481-483, 1966b.

Koppitz EM. Emotional indicators on human figure drawings of shy and aggressive children. *Journal of Clinical Psychology,* 22, 466-469, 1966c.

Koppitz EM. Expected and exceptional items of human figure drawings and IQ scores of children age 5 to 12. *Journal of Clinical Psychology,* 23, 81-83, 1967.

Koppitz EM. *Psychological evaluation of children's human figure drawings.* New York, Grune and Stratton, 1968.

Koppitz EM. *Psychological evaluation of human figure drawings by middle school pupils.* New York: Grune and Stratton, 1984.

Leaman KM. Sexual abuse: The reactions of child and family. In K. MacFarlane, B. Jones and L. Jenstrom (Eds.) *Sexual abuse of children: Selected readings.* Washington, DC: National Center on Child Abuse and Neglect, OHDS, U.S. DHHS, 21-24, 1980.

Levy S. Projective figure drawing. In E.F. Hammer (Ed.), *The clinical application of projective drawings.* Springfield, IL: Thomas, 83-112, 1958.

Lowenfield V. *The nature of creative activity.* New York: MacMillan, l939.

Luscher M. *The Luscher Color Test.* New York: Simon and Schuster, 1969.

MacFarland K. and Waterman J. *Sexual abuse of young children: Evaluation and treatment.* New York: Guilford Press, 1986.

Machover K. *Personality projection in the drawing of the human figure: A method of personality investigation.* Springfield, IL: Thomas, 1949.

Machover K. Human figure drawings of children. *Journal of Projective Techniques,* 17, 85-91, 1953.

Machover K. The body image in art communication as seen in William Steig's drawings. *Journal of Projective Techniques,* 19, 453-460, 1955.

Machover K. Sex differences in the developmental pattern of children as seen in human figure drawings. In AL. Rabin and MR. Haworth (Eds.), *Projective techniques with children.* New York: Grune and Stratton, 238-257, 1960.

Martin J., Anderson J., Romans S., Mullen P. and O'Shea M. Asking about child sexual abuse: Methodological implications of a two-stage survey. *Child Abuse and Neglect,* 17, 383-92, l993.

Meiselman K. *Incest: A psychological study of causes and effects with treatment recommendations.* San Francisco: Jossey-Bass, 1978.

Meyers DV. Toward an objective evaluation procedure of the kinetic family drawing. *Journal of Personality Assessment, 42,* 358-365, 1978.

Miller A. *The drama of the gifted child.* New York: Basic Books, 1981.

Mostkoff D. and Lazarus P. The kinetic family drawing: The reliability of an objective scoring system. *Psychology in the Schools, 20,* 16-20, 1983.

Osler G. and Gould P. *Using drawing in assessment and therapy: A guide for mental health professionals.* New York: Brunner/Mazel, 1987.

Palmer JO. *The psychological assessment of children* (2nd ed.). New York: John Wiley and Sons, 1983.

Papadakis-Michaelides EA. Unpublished dissertation, University of Birmingham, 1989.

Peters JJ. Children who are victims of sexual assault and the psychology of offenders. *American Journal of Psychotherapy,* 30, 398-421, 1976.

Peterson LW. Use of art in the assessment and treatment of children in wartime. In JE. Lundeberg, U. Otto and B. Rybeck (Eds.), *Wartime medical services.* Second International Conference, Stockholm, Sweden: 120-129, 1990.

Peterson LW., Hardin ME., and Nitsch MJ. The use of children's drawings in the evaluation and treatment of child sexual, emotional, and physical abuse. *Archives of Family Medicine,* 4, 445-452, 1995.

Peterson LW., Nitsch MJ. and Higgins PA. Therapeutic program for bereaved children. *Archives of Family Medicine,* 3, 76-83, 1994.

Peterson LW. and Rahe RH. Using family life drawings in medical student education. *Family Medicine,* 23(8), 603-608, 1991.

Reno Gazette-Journal. *Heather's story: A brief and violent journey,* 1, 14, August 21, 1988.

Reno Gazette-Journal. *Girl draws project at mail bombing trial,* 1B, May 7, 1994.

Ricci C. *L'Arte dei Bambini.* Bologna: N. Zanichelli, 1887.

Robinson M. Interviewing children as an assessment tool. In K. Babich (Ed.), *Assessing the mental health of children,* Western Interstate Commission for Higher Education Conference, Denver: 59-71, 1982.

Sayed AJ. and Leaverton DR. Kinetic-family-drawings of children with diabetes. *Child Psychiatry and Human Development,* 5(1), 40-50, 1974.

Schaie K. and Heiss L. *Color and personality: A manual for the color pyramid test,* Hans Huber, 1964.

Sgroi SM. *Vulnerable populations: Evaluation and treatment of sexually abused children and adult survivors.* Lexington, MA: Lexington Books, 1982.

Spencer MJ. and Dunklee P. Sexual abuse of boys. *Pediatrics,* 78, 133-8, 1986.

Steiner M. and Peterson L. Severe emotional response to eye trauma in a child: Awareness and intervention. *Archives of Ophthalmology,* 110, 753, 1992.

Summit R. The child sexual abuse accommodation syndrome. *Child Abuse and Neglect,* 7, 177-193, 1983.

Sundbert N. The practice of psychological testing in clinical services throughout the United States. *American Psychologist,* 16, 79-83, 1961.

Swenson CH. Empirical evaluations of human figure drawings: 1957-1966. *Psychological Bulletin,* 70, 20-44, 1968.

Terr L. Forbidden games: Post-traumatic child's play. *Journal of American Academy of Child Psychiatry,* 20, 741-760, 1981.

Terr L. Chowchilla revisited: The effects of psychic trauma four years after a school bus kidnapping. *American Journal of Psychiatry,* 140, 1543-1550, 1983.

Terr L. *Too scared to cry.* New York: Harper and Row, 1991.

Vandeven AM. and Emans SJ. Sexual abuse of children and adolescents. *Current Opinion in Obstetrics and Gynecology,* 4, 843-848, 1992.

VanderMey BJ. The sexual victimization of male children: A review of previous research. *Child Abuse and Neglect,* 12, 61-72, 1988.

van der Kolk BA. The trauma spectrum: The interaction of biological and social events in the genesis of trauma response. *Journal of Traumatic Stress,* 273-290, 1988.

van der Kolk BA. The behavioral and psychobiological effects of developmental trauma. In A. Stoudemire (Ed.), *Human Behavior: An introduction for medial students.* Philadelphia: JB Lippincott, 328-343, 1994.

Vane JR. and Eisen VW. The Goodenough Draw-A-Person Test and signs of maladjustment in kindergarten children. *Journal of Clinical Psychology,* 18, 276-279, 1962.

Volavkova H. (Ed.). *I never saw another butterfly: Children's drawings and poems from Terezin concentration camp 1942-1944.* New York: Schocken Books, 1978.

Waterman J., Kelley RJ., Oliveri MK. and McCord, J. *Behind the playground walls: Sexual abuse in preschools.* New York: Guilford Press, 1993.

Wilkins R. Women who sexually abuse children. *BMJ,* 300, 1153-4, 1990.

Wohl A. and Kaufman B. *Silent screams and hidden cries: An interpretation of art work by children from violent homes.* New York: Brunner/Mazel, 1985.

Yates A., Beutler LE. and Crago M. Drawings by child victims of incest. *Child Abuse and Neglect,* 9, 183-189, 1985.

Yornberger W. *Fire from the sky: Salvadoran children's drawings.* New York: Writers and Readers Publishing Cooperative, 1986.

APPENDIX A

EXPECTED AND EXCEPTIONAL DEVELOPMENTAL ITEMS ON HUMAN FIGURE DRAWINGS OF BOYS AND GIRLS AGE 5 –12

EXPECTED ITEMS	Age 5 Boys	Age 5 Girls	Age 6 Boys	Age 6 Girls	Age 7 Boys	Age 7 Girls	Age 8 Boys	Age 8 Girls	Age 9 Boys	Age 9 Girls	Age 10 Boys	Age 10 Girls	Ages 11 and 12 Boys	Ages 11 and 12 Girls
N	128	128	131	133	134	125	138	130	134	134	109	108	157	167
Head	X	X	X	X	X	X	X	X	X	X	X	X	X	X
Eyes	X	X	X	X	X	X	X	X	X	X	X	X	X	X
Nose	X	X	X	X	X	X	X	X	X	X	X	X	X	X
Mouth	X	X	X	X	X	X	X	X	X	X	X	X	X	X
Body	X	X	X	X	X	X	X	X	X	X	X	X	X	X
Legs	X	X	X	X	X	X	X	X	X	X	X	X	X	X
Arms		X	X	X	X	X	X	X	X	X	X	X	X	X
Feet				X	X	X	X	X	X	X	X	X	X	X
Arms 2-dimension					X	X	X	X	X	X	X	X	X	X
Legs 2-dimension						X		X		X	X	X	X	X
Hair				X		X	X	X	X	X	X	X	X	X
Neck						X		X		X	X	X	X	X
Arm down													X	
Arms at shoulder														X
2 clothing items												X		X

EXCEPTIONAL ITEMS	Age 5 Boys	Age 5 Girls	Age 6 Boys	Age 6 Girls	Age 7 Boys	Age 7 Girls	Age 8 Boys	Age 8 Girls	Age 9 Boys	Age 9 Girls	Age 10 Boys	Age 10 Girls	Ages 11 and 12 Boys	Ages 11 and 12 Girls
Knee	X	X	X	X	X	X	X	X	X	X	X	X	X	X
Profile	X	X	X	X	X	X	X	X	X	X		X		
Elbows	X	X	X	X	X	X	X	X	X					
Two lips	X	X	X	X	X	X	X		X		X			
Nostrils	X	X	X	X	X		X		X					
Proportions	X	X	X	X	X									
Arms at shoulder	X	X	X	X										
4 clothing items	X	X	X	X										
Feet 2-dimensions	X	X												
Five fingers	X													
Pupils	X													

Data from Koppitz, 1967

APPENDIX B

HUMAN FIGURE DRAWING RESEARCH BY MILTON HARDIN

This HFD drawing inventory is based in part on Hardin's (1989) analysis of 842 children's drawings. This research included a total of 341 children who had been sexually molested; 252 children who were clinic-referred but determined not to have been sexually molested; and 249 children who were from the general population grades K-4. Ages for the subjects were 6-10 years (211 were 6 years; 164 were 7 years; 158 were 8 years; 158 were 9 years; and 151 were 10 years of age). There were 353 males and 489 females. It is important to note that sexually molested children were positively diagnosed by a physician and therapist evaluator, whereas the normal population was not screened for sexual or emotional problems. Thus the normal classroom population may have contained some children undiagnosed for sexual or emotional conditions resulting in a % of indicator for "normal" children that is higher than it might actually be if the school population had been screened. Children in the group referred to clinics were assessed for emotional problems; physical and sexual abuse had been ruled out. The following table presents by indicator the actual and percentile ratings for each designated category of children.

INDICATOR	MOLESTED (%)	CLINIC (%)	GENERAL (%)	TOTAL (%)
1. Genitals/Explicit	54 (15.8)	1 (0.4)	1 (0.4)	56 (6.7)
2. Genitals/Concealment	50 (14.7)	11 (4.4)	16 (6.4)	77 (9.1)
3. Genitals/Omission	34 (10.0)	7 (2 8)	12 (4.8)	53 (6.3)
4. Belly Button	34 (10.0)	9 (3.6)	5 (2.0)	48 (5.7)
5. Encapsulation	144 (42.2)	40 (15.9)	35 (14.1)	219 (26.0)
6. Fruit Trees	46 (13.5)	9 (3.6)	9 (3.6)	64 (7.6)
7. Opposite Sex Drawn	100 (29.3)	47 (18.7)	24 (9.6)	171 (20.3)
8. Tiny Figure	161 (47.2)	139 (55.2)	75 (30.1)	375 (44.5)
9. Head Shading	62 (18.2)	40 (15.9)	86 (34.5)	188 (22.3)
10. Distortion	234 (68.6)	168 (66.7)	141 (56.6)	543 (64.5)
11. Hands/Cut off	91 (26.7)	62 (24.6)	34 (13.7)	181 (22.2)
12. Omission-Peripheral	49 (14.4)	40 (15.9)	7 (2.8)	96 (11.4)
13. Big Hands	103 (30.2)	77 (30.6)	71 (28.5)	251 (29.8)
14. Slanting Figure	88 (25.8)	69 (27.4)	59 (23.7)	216 (25.7)
15. Genitals/Emphasis	35 (10.3)	11 (4.4)	25 (10.0)	71 (8.4)
16. Belt/Waistband	40 (11.7)	28 (11.1)	49 (19.7)	117 (13.9)
17. Legs Together	42 (12.3)	21 (8.3)	25 (10.0)	88 (10.5)
18. Transparency	42 (12.3)	18 (7.1)	18 (7.2)	78 (9.3)
19. Rainbows	29 (8.5)	3 (1.2)	5 (2.0)	37 (4.4)
20. Butterflies	15 (4.4)	1 (0.4)	2 (0.8)	18 (2.1)
21. Hearts	44 (12.9)	12 (4.8)	23 (9.2)	79 (9.4)
22. Flying Birds	18 (5.3)	4 (1.6)	3 (1.2)	25 (3.0)
23. X's on Body Parts	63 (18.5)	52 (20.6)	76 (30.5)	191 (22.7)
24. Smudging Face	63 (18.5)	48 (19.0)	108 (43.4)	219 (26.0)
25. Body Shading	93 (27.3)	65 (25.8)	79 (31.7)	237 (28.1)
26. Nose/Emphasis	103 (30.2)	60 (23.8)	88 (35.3)	251 (29.8)
27. Hair/Emphasis	170 (49.9)	107 (42.5)	129 (51.8)	406 (48.2)
28. "O"-Mouth Emphasis	51 (15.0)	21 (8.3)	45 (18.1)	117 (13.9)
29. Kites	1 (0.3)	4 (1.6)	2 (0 8)	7 (0.8)
30. Balloons	10 (2.9)	5 (2.0)	8 (3.2)	23 (2.7)
31. Waist/Cut off	26 (7.6)	15 (6.0)	7 (2.8)	48 (5.7)
32. Omission-Central	45 (13.2)	22 (8.7)	4 (1.6)	71 (8.4)
33. Circling Body Parts	182 (53.4)	112 (44.4)	152 (61.0)	446 (53.0)

APPENDIX C

COMPARISON OF KOPPITZ AND HARDIN INDICATORS

KOPPITZ (1968)	HARDIN (1989–90)
1. Poor integration of parts	Coded as "Distortion"
2. Shading of face	Coded as "Shading-Head"
3. Shading of body and/or limbs	Coded as "Shading-Body"
4. Shading of hands and/or neck	Coded as "Shading-Body"
5. Gross asymmetry of limbs	Coded as "Distortion"
6. Slanting figure >15°	Coded the same
7. Tiny figure	Coded the same
8. Big figure	Not Studied
9. Transparencies	Coded the same
10. Tiny head	Not studied
11. Crossed eyes	Not studied
12. Teeth	Not studied
13. Short arms	Not studied
14. Long arms	Not studied
15. Arms clinging to body	Not studied
16. Big hands	Coded the same
17. Hands cut off	Coded the same
18. Legs pressed together	Coded as "Legs tightly together"
19. Genitals	Coded as "Explicit drawing of genitalia"; "Concealment of genitalia"; "Omission of genital area"; "Genitals emphasized"
20. Monster or grotesque figure	Coded as "Distortion"
21. Three or more figures	Not studied
22. Clouds	Not studied
23. No eyes	Not studied
24. No nose	Not studied
25. No mouth	Not studied
26. No body	Coded as "Omission of central part of figure"
27. No arms	Coded as "Omission of peripheral body parts"
28. No legs	Coded as "Omission of peripheral body parts"
29. No feet	Not studied
30. No neck	Not studied

APPENDIX D

RESULTS OF MILTON HARDIN'S RESEARCH (1989–90) ON THE SCREENING INVENTORY FOR CHILD HUMAN FIGURE DRAWINGS

I.   Red Level: "Serious Seven"

The following indicators were found by Hardin in 1989 to significantly differentiate sexually abused from non-abused children when a factor analysis was done comparing the scores of 842 children ages 6-10 in three groups: (1) positively identified as sexually molested (341 children); (2) positively not molested but having emotional and behavioral problems (252 children); (3) "general population" children not identified as having sexual molest or emotional problems but possibly containing non-identifiable features (249 children). Inter-rater reliability in scoring was .80.

Indicator

1. **Explicit Drawing of Genitals.** Hardin found 15.8% of molested children did this in their HFDs. Less than 0.5% of all other children, including the clinical referred group did this in HFDs. It is important to note that this was more often done by molested children who were 6 and 7 years old. Older children (molested) rarely did this in HFDs. There were no gender differences for this sexual indicator (Hardin, 1989; Koppitz, 1968).

2. **Concealment of Genitals.** Hardin found 14.7% of molested children did this in HFDs. All other children did this less than 6.5% of the time. It is important to note that older molested children did this more than younger molested children, especially 9 and 10 year olds. We imagine that older molested children would be more sophisticated in their drawings and less obvious than younger children. Older molested children might also feel more guilt and anxiety, and therefore be prone to concealment. There were no statistically significant gender differences, although females tended to do this more often than males (Hardin, 1989).

3. **Omission of Genital Regions.** Hardin found 10% of all molested children did this in HFDs. All other children did this less than 5% of the time. There were no significant age or gender differences. Omissions may be a method of avoidance (Hardin, 1989).

4. **Omission of Central Part of Figure.** Hardin found 13.2% of molested children did this in HFDs; 8.7% of the clinic-referred group did this and only 1.6% of the general population group did this. These central omissions were emotional indicators, as well as moderate molest indicators. A significant number of 6-year-olds (all groups) did this. Thus it was a much stronger indicator for 7-year-olds and up. Males were more likely than females to do this in their drawings (Hardin 1989).

5. **Encapsulation of the HFD.** Hardin found 42.2% of all molested children did this in HFDs. It was important to note that 14.1% of the general population and 15.9% of clinic-referred children also did this in their HFDs. These numbers are relatively high, but 42.2% was significantly different from the other two groups. There were no age or gender differences (Hardin, 1989).

6. **Fruit Trees Added.** Hardin found this to be one of the most unexpected findings. These types of trees were added by the child. It was usually an apple or cherry tree, but any fruit tree would do. 13.5% of molested children did this in HFDs, and 3.6% of all other children added these to HFDs. Molested females were more likely to do this. There were no age differences (Hardin, 1989).

7. **Opposite Sex from the Child is Drawn.** Hardin found this indicator to be critical for sexual molestation and emotional distress. 29.3% of molested children did this, and 18.7% of clinic-referred children did this, but only 9.6% of children in the general population did this. For whatever reasons, drawing a figure that was the opposite sex when the child was asked to draw "a person" was significant. The instructions said: "Draw me a person," not "Draw me a man," or "Draw yourself." There was a little less tendency to do this as children got older. There was also a very significant gender difference. Many more females did this than males (Hardin, 1989).

APPENDIX D (continued)

The following indicators were included in the Hardin Study and taken directly from the research of Koppitz, Osler, Gould and Jolles. Although these indicators did not significantly differentiate sexually abused children, the indicators are included in the Hardin/Peterson inventory due to their clinical utility and long quantitative research history. The following data show the % of indicators which appeared in the Hardin sample of molested, emotionally distressed, and normal non-screened children.

8. **Tiny Figure.** Hardin found this in 55.2% of the clinic-referred group, 47.2% of the sexually molested group, and 30% of the general population. This indicator occurred frequently, but there were statistical differences between the groups. No age or gender differences were found. Because of the high numbers in all groups, a tiny figure was considered a mild to moderate emotional indicator. A Koppitz indicator (Koppitz, 1968; Osler & Gould, 1987).

9. **Poor Integration of Body Parts/Monster Drawn.** Hardin coded these indicators as "distortion" which included poor integration, gross assembly of limbs, monster or grotesque figure. In the Hardin study, 68.6 % of sexually molested, 66.7% of clinic-referred, and 56.6% of the general population of a total of 64.5% of all children drew these indicators. Because it occurred in over 50% of children, it could not be called a cinical indicator. This may be due to the inclusion of too many indicators in one heading (Koppitz, 1968; Osler & Gould, 1987).

10. **Hands Cut Off.** Hardin found 24.6% of clinic referred and 26.7% of molested children did this in HFDs; 13.7% of the general population did this in HFDs. Younger children did this more often and it decreased with age. This was considered a moderate to critical emotional indicator by Koppitz (1968); and Osler & Gould (1987).

11. **Omission of Peripheral Part of Figure.** Hardin found 15.9% of clinic-referred and 14.4% of molested children did this in HFDs. Only 2.8% of the general population did this in HFDs. There was a significant age difference. Young children did this much more often than older children. This was considered to be a critical emotional indicator, especially for children over 7 years old. Females did this a little more than males (Koppitz, 1968; Jolles, 1971).

12. **Belly Button Added or Emphasized.** Hardin found 10% of molested children did this in HFDs. Less than 3.6% of all other children did this in HFD's. Addition of a belly button was more common in young (6-year-old) molested children and in HFD's of molested females. It is possible that what was perceived as a "belly button" in the HFD's may have been intended to be a vagina (therefore, an explicit drawing of genitalia).

13. **Jagged Teeth.** Not a Hardin indicator (Koppitz, 1968; Osler & Gould, 1987).

14. **Big Hands.** Hardin found 30.2% of molested, 30.% of the clinic group, and 28.% of the general population did this in HFD's. It was found significant by Koppitz (1968), Osler & Gould (1987), and Peterson, Nitsch & Higgins (1994). It was not found to discriminate aggression by Cox (1993) or to be discriminative for Hardin's population (Hardin, 1989)

15. **Transparency.** Hardin found 12.3% of molested children did this with HFDs; 7.2% of other children did this in their drawings. This quality was not necessarily indicative of molestation, but a moderate trend toward suggestivity existed, especially in conjunction with other sexual molest indicators. There were no age or gender differences. This is also a Koppitz (1968) indicator.

APPENDIX D (continued)

II. Yellow Level: "Suspicious Five"

Indicator

1. **Slanting Figure.** Hardin found 25.% of the molested children, 27.4% of the clinic-referred children, and 23.7% of the general population did this in HFDs. In the Hardin study the figure had to be 15° from vertical (Koppitz, 1968; Peterson, Nitsch & Higgins, 1994).

2. **Genitals Emphasized.** Hardin found 10.3% of molested children did this in HFDs; 10% of children in the general population did this in HFDs; but only 4.4% of the group referred to clinics did this in HFDs. In the Hardin study, the clinic-referred group was screened for molestation. It is probably safe to say that the general population had molested children who had not been identified by authorities or professionals. That is why some of the sexual molest indicators may have been higher in the general population group than in the group referred to clinics.

3. **Legs Tightly Together.** Hardin found 12.3% of molested children did this, whereas 8.3% of the group referred to clinics did this in HFDs. It is important to note that 10% of children in the general population did this also. Ten-year-old children did this much more than all other ages. Females did this in HFDs more than males.

4. **Waist Cut Off.** Hardin found 6.0% of the clinic referred and 7.6% of the molested children did this in HFDs; 2.8% of the general population did this. As children got older, they did this less often in drawings. There were no gender differences (Hardin, 1989).

5. **Extensions.** This was not a Hardin indicator. It was described by Burns & Kaufman (1972) and described as "long arms" by Koppitz (1968).

The following indicators have been found to appear in the drawings of molested and emotionally troubled children. There is less research evidence and more clinical evidence for their inclusion in the inventory. The clinician should not overinterpret these indicators.

6. **Rainbows.** Hardin found 8.5% of molested children spontaneously added rainbows to their HFDs; 1.2% of the clinic group and 2.0% of the general population did this in HFDs. There were no age differences. Females did this more than males.

7. **Butterflies.** Hardin found 4.4% of molested children added butterflies to HFDs. Less than 0.8% of all other children did this in HFDs. Obviously, this does not occur often, but when it does, it could be significant. Older children did this much more often than younger children. There were no gender differences (Hardin, 1989).

8. **Hearts.** Hardin found 12.9% of molested children added hearts to HFDs; 9.2% of the general population did this, as well. Only 4.8% of the clinic-referred group did this in HFDs. There was a definite gender difference for this sexual molest indicator. Only 2% of males did this, while 14.7% of females did this in HFDs. Therefore, hearts in male HFDs should be looked at as a more significant finding (Hardin, 1989).

APPENDIX D (continued)

9. **Flying Birds.** Hardin found 5.3% of molested children added flying birds to HFDs. Less than 1.6% of all other children did this in HFDs. There were no age or gender differences (Hardin, 1989).

10. **Rain/Clouds.** This was not a Hardin indicator, but a traditional Koppitz indicator.

11. **Shading of Face.** This was a Hardin indicator showing up in18.2% of the sexually molested, 15.9% of the clinic population, and 34.5% of the general population. This is a traditional Koppitz indicator; however, Hardin found it to be a "positive indicator" that appears more often in the general poplulation than in clinic or molested children (Hardin, 1989; Kopppitz, 1968).

12. **Unicorns.** This was not a Hardin indicator; however, it has been informally noted by clinicians working with molested children.

13. **Jagged Teeth.** This was not a Hardin indicator; however, it has been reported with physically abused children (Koppitz 1968, Osler & Gould 1987).

14. **X for Eyes.** This was not a Hardin indicator; however, it has been reported by clinicians working with physically abused children.

Inter-rater reliability for the Hardin study was 0.80 using three raters. The original 33 indicators for the Hardin study were selected from a review of the enduring art research for quantitative emotional indicators (Koppitz) and interviews with child sexual abuse therapists and national research experts who publish their work with sexually abused children. The drawings collected from 842 children were completed at the initial assessment for sexual abuse. The drawings were only one of the intake procedures. All children were screened to have no prior history of therapy. The pictures used in the study were looked at retrospectively after positive identification had been made for sexual abuse. The drawings from the emotionally disturbed were retrospectively examined after sexual abuse was ruled out. In the case of normal children, a teacher collected the drawings, which were then evaluated by the researchers.

APPENDIX E

K-F-D ANALYSIS

Name: _____   Age: ____   Sex: ____

I. STYLE(S) (Circle)

A. Compartmentalization
B. Edging
C. Encapsulation
D. Folded Compartmentalization
E. Lining on the Bottom
F. Lining on the Top
G. Underlining Individual Figures

II. SYMBOL(S)

A. _____   D. _____
B. _____   E. _____
C. _____   F. _____

III. (A) ACTIONS OF INDIVIDUAL FIGURES

Figure	Action
1. Self	_____
2. Mother	_____
3. Father	_____
4. Older Brother	_____
5. Older Sister	_____
6. Younger Brother	_____
7. Younger Sister	_____
8. Other (Specify)	_____

(B) ACTIONS BETWEEN INDIVIDUAL FIGURES

Figure	Action	Recipient
1. Self	_____	_____
2. Mother	_____	_____
3. Father	_____	_____
4. Older Brother	_____	_____
5. Older Sister	_____	_____
6. Younger Brother	_____	_____
7. Younger Sister	_____	_____
8. Other (Specify)	_____	_____

IV. CHARACTERISTICS OF INDIVIDUAL K-F-D FIGURES

A. Arm Extensions
1. Self   5. O.S.
2. Mother   6. Y.B.
3. Father   7. Y.S.
4. O.B.   8. Other

B. Elevated Figures
1. Self   5. O.S.
2. Mother   6. Y.B.
3. Father   7. Y.S.
4. O.B.   8. Other

C. Erasures
1. Self   5. O.S.
2. Mother   6. Y.B.
3. Father   7. Y.S.
4. O.B.   8. Other

D. Figures on Back
1. Self   5. O.S.
2. Mother   6. Y.B.
3. Father   7. Y.S.
4. O.B.   8. Other

E. Hanging
1. Self   5. O.S.
2. Mother   6. Y.B.
3. Father   7. Y.S.
4. O.B.   8. Other

F. Omission of Body Parts
1. Self   5. O.S.
2. Mother   6. Y.B.
3. Father   7. Y.S.
4. O.B.   8. Other

G. Omission of Figures
1. Self   5. O.S.
2. Mother   6. Y.B.
3. Father   7. Y.S.
4. O.B.   8. Other

H. Picasso Eye
1. Self   5. O.S.
2. Mother   6. Y.B.
3. Father   7. Y.S.
4. O.B.   8. Other

I. Rotated Figures
1. Self   5. O.S.
2. Mother   6. Y.B.
3. Father   7. Y.S.
4. O.B.   8. Other

V. K-F-D GRID

A. Height
1. Self   4. O.B.   7. Y.S.
2. Mother   5. O.S.   8. Other
3. Father   6. Y.B.

B. Location of Self

C. Distance of Self from:

Mother _____
Father _____
Other _____

Data from Burns & Kaufman, 1970, 1972

APPENDIX F
HUMAN FIGURE DRAWING INDICATOR MEANINGS

RED INDICATORS	MEANING
1. **Explicit genitalia**	Strongest indicator for sexual molestation in young children (Hardin, 1989). Less frequent as children get older (Koppitz, 1968). (Cultural and artistic variables should be considered.)
2. **Concealment of genitalia** 3. **Omission of genital area** 4. **Omission of central part of figure**	Indicators 2, 3 & 4 are sexual molestation indicators drawn most often by older children who are more sophisticated and wish to deny or cover up abuse. For younger children this may be appropriate (i.e., tadpole figure) (Hardin, 1989).
5. **Encapsulation of drawing**	Feeling isolated, fearful, need to provide self with a barrier to the world, or self protection (Hardin, 1989).
6. **Fruit trees spontaneously added**	13.5% of molested children draw these, whereas only 3.6% of normal or clinic referred children draw fruit trees (Hardin, 1989).
7. **Opposite sex drawn**	Can reflect sexual confusion or sexual identity problem. Reflection of person drawn, likes or dislikes. Multi-determined by personality factors, cultrual factors, situational stress. Also seen in molested children (Hardin, 1989).
8. **Tiny figure**	Insecurity or lack of power (Koppitz, 1968; Osler & Gould, 1987).
9. **Poor integration of body parts/ monster depictions**	Rule out perceptual and motor abilities. Seen normally in children with muscular dystrophy. When above conditions are ruled out, check emotional problems or physical abuse (Koppitz, 1968; Osler & Gould, 1987).
10. **Hands cut off**	Lack of control, powerless. Hands represent ability to affect the world (Koppitz, 1968; Osler & Gould, 1987).
11. **Omission of arms or legs**	Incapacitated. Helpless, hopeless. Qualitatively more serious than #10. Inability to move in or out of a situation (Koppitz, 1968; Jolles, 1971).
12. **Belly button added or emphasized**	This is a sexual molest indicator of younger children. More commonly drawn by females (could be mistaken for a vagina) (Hardin, 1989).
13. **Jagged teeth**	Aggressive person, severe rivalry, physical abuse (Koppitz, 1968; Osler & Gould, 1987).
14. **Big hands**	Aggressive, poor impulse control (Koppitz, 1968; Osler & Gould, 1987; Peterson, Nitsch & Higgins, 1994).
15. **Transparency**	Severely disturbed, or confused about body parts. Possible molest. "People can see through me." Privacy invaded. "Body not my own" (Koppitz, 1968).

APPENDIX F (continued)

YELLOW INDICATORS	MEANING
1. **Slanting figure**	Something is out of balance. Disequilibrium. The more the slant, the more unstable. Drawn normally by dyslexic children. Seen in pictures of bereaved children representing deceased (Koppitz, 1968; Peterson, Nitsch & Higgins, 1994).
2. **Genitals emphasized**	Noted in older molested children. Similar to concealment of genitalia, but done too frequently by normal children to be predictive of molestation (Hardin, 1989)
3. **Legs tightly together**	Stuck, unable to move. Mild indicator of molestation (Koppitz, 1968; Hardin, 1989).
4. **Waist cut off**	Denial. Withholding. "Nothing below the waist exists" (Hardin, 1989).
5. **Extensions**	Holding the world at a distance. Withdrawn or suspicious children (Burns & Kaufman, 1972).
6. **Rainbows**	Rainbows can be an elaborate encapsulation (Hardin, 1989).
7. **Butterflies** 8. **Hearts** 9. **Flying birds**	Indicators 7, 8, 9 are an attempt to "put on a happy face" and are added spontaneously by children with physical or sexual abuse issues or emotional problems. These are the most "subtle" of child communication signals. The picture looks to the adult as happy, when in fact the child is trying hard to pretend he or she is happy (Hardin, 1989).
10. **Rain/Clouds**	Note how drawn as well as how extensive on the page. Usually associated with sadness or depression (Koppitz, 1968),
11. **Shading of face**	Shame, depression, anxiety or embarrassment (Koppitz, 1968; Osler & Gould, 1987, Peterson, Nitsch & Higgins, 1994).
12. **Unicorns**	Mild indicator for molestation. Phallic symbol. Drawn too frequently by normal children (especially females) to be red indicator. Use interview guide or ask to draw another picture.

APPENDIX G
KINETIC FAMILY DRAWING INDICATOR MEANINGS

I. QUALITY OF OVERALL DRAWING

Peculiarity

The drawing will have an odd or strange aspect. This is a method the child may use to avoid the task such as drawing a dinosaur rather than a family. Look at accidents or errors or odd productions as a way of hiding or avoiding. Ask the child to do another drawing.

Feeling/Mood

Is the picture happy, sad, fearful? How would it feel to be there? How does it feel to view?

Order

This relates to consistency or inconsistency in an individual's family life. May also reflect the degree of organization or disorganization.

II. CHILD PERCEPTION OF FAMILY MEMBERS

Size

Does it represent reality? Power or lack of power? Value or devaluation? (Lowenfeld, 1939; Cox, 1993).

Shape

Disproportion in shape represents a possible problem area with a family member.

Distortion

Distortion may represent a cognitive deficit. It may also indicate a child's true perception of reality such as a physical or motoric disability. It can, finally, be an indicator of physical or sexual abuse.

III. CHILD SELF-PERCEPTION IN FAMILY SYSTEM

Size

Child's size in relation to the family members. Does it represent reality? Power or lack of power? Value or devaluation? (Lowenfeld, 1939; Cox, 1993).

Shape

Child's shape in relation to the other family members. Does it represent reality? Disproportions in shape represent problem areas. Children with asthma for example may draw an enlarged nose.

Distortion

Child's body part(s) significantly different from family members'. Does it represent reality? Distortion may represent a cognitive deficit. It may also indicate a child's true perception of reality such as in muscular dystrophy. Finally, it can be an indicator of physical or sexual abuse.

APPENDIX G (continued)

IV. STYLES

Encapsulation	The need to draw specific boundaries around oneself, to set one-self apart from others.
Compartmentalization	Boxes or compartments around each family member or specific member or self. Protection or distancing needed.
Writing words on picture	The child may need to make sure the drawing is understood. Labeling people or objects may be a way of maintaining control or getting the point across to the viewer.
Edging	Indicative of denying or covering up. Partially involved but not committed.
Underlining individual figures	An underscored figure usually denotes grounding. However, if all figures except this one are underlined, that one is usually grounded.
Lining at top of paper	Fear associated with a "burden carried over one's head" that a person feels a need to control but unable to control.
Lining at bottom of paper	Emphasis or stability.

V. TREATMENT OF FIGURES

Transparency	Seeing through a wall or person or clothing or skin to bone. Often represents a taboo area, such as sexuality. No boundaries. Body doesn't belong to self.
Missing person or self	Observe who is absent or left out of the picture. If the self is deleted, the child may perceive he is an outsider or left out of the family. A missing person may represent someone who is absent from the person's life or the family system. Observe who is removed or moved out of sight. This is often a sign of conflict with the missing person.
One or more figures drawn on back of paper	May indicate unstable person or individual leaving the family (divorce) or dying (deceased).
Erasures	Note erasures and compare redrawn work. These frequently represent conflict areas or persons.
Floating	Out of control. Nothing to hang on to.
Hanging	Fearful, lack of control, upside down.
Falling	Out of control. Nothing to hang on to.
Slanting figures	Instability. The more slant, the more unstable.
Incomplete figures	Who has power and who lacks power?
Extensions/Long legs, arms, equipment	A device drawn in the hand of a figure to provide a barrier or hold a person at a distance, such as long hands or extensions or sports equipment such as racquets or bats. Person can either see self as powerful or wanting more power.

APPENDIX G (continued)

IV. ACTIONS WITH NEGATIVE ASPECTS

Sexualized	How are genitalia expressed: explicit, omitted, exagerated, concealed?
Aggression/Weapons	Note direction of aggression to determine potential violence.
Fear/Anxiety	Who is fearful and scared?
Withdrawal/Isolation	Note who is isolated and why?
Blame/Ridicule	Who is blaming?
Submission/Competition	Who is requiring submission? Who is competitive?
Barriers	Who is blocking whom from communicating or creating barriers? Who is the child protecting him or herself from by drawing a barrier?

Notes